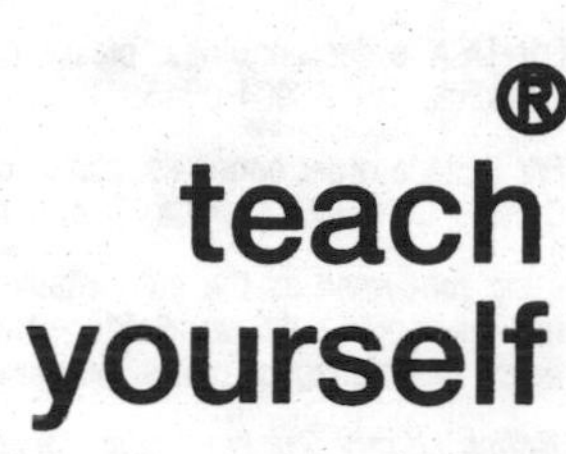

managing IT for small businesses

michael pagan

for over 60 years, more than 50 million people have learnt over 750 subjects the **teach yourself** way, with impressive results.

be where you want to be with **teach yourself**

For UK order enquiries: please contact Bookpoint Ltd, 130 Milton Park, Abingdon, Oxon OX14 4SB. Telephone: +44 (0)1235 827720. Fax: +44 (0)1235 400454. Lines are open 09.00–17.00, Monday to Saturday, with a 24-hour message answering service. Details about our titles and how to order are available at www.teachyourself.co.uk.

For USA order enquiries: please contact McGraw-Hill Customer Services, PO Box 545, Blacklick, OH 43004-0545, USA. Telephone: 1-800-722-4726. Fax: 1-614-755-5645.

For Canada order enquiries: please contact McGraw-Hill Ryerson Ltd, 300 Water St, Whitby, Ontario L1N 9B6, Canada. Telephone: 905 430 5000. Fax: 905 430 5020.

Long renowned as the authoritative source for self-guided learning – with more than 50 million copies sold worldwide – the **teach yourself** series includes over 500 titles in the fields of languages, crafts, hobbies, business, computing and education.

British Library Cataloguing in Publication Data: a catalogue record for this title is available from The British Library.

Library of Congress Catalog Card Number: on file.

First published in UK 2007 by Hodder Education, 338 Euston Road, London NW1 3BH.

First published in US 2007 by The McGraw-Hill Companies, Inc.

Typeset by MacDesign, Southampton

Printed in Great Britain for Hodder Education, a division of Hodder Headline, an Hachette Livre UK Company, 338 Euston Road, London NW1 3BH, by Cox & Wyman Ltd, Reading, Berkshire.

Impression number 10 9 8 7 6 5 4 3 2 1

Year 2011 2010 2009 2008 2007

contents

Dedication

To my wife Ali for her tireless support and help.

Acknowledgements

This book came about from my frustration at business managers and IT people behaving as though they were on separate planets (there were some honourable exceptions). This resulted in a training course aimed at bridging the gap between '*those who understand what they do not manage, and those who manage what they do not understand*'. From that course came this book. Thanks to all who gave support, especially to Kevin Duncan for his encouragement and advice.

With regard to the case study, The Coffee Company, on pages 58–61: these materials are reproduced with the express permission of the Victorian Government, Australia, as owner of the copyright.

introduction

Technology is dominated by two types of people: those who understand what they do not manage, and those who manage what they do not understand.

Anonymous

There is an old saying that companies know that 50 per cent of their advertising is a waste of money but don't know which 50 per cent. This is equally true for IT. Middle and senior managers are unsure about IT but need to make strategic decisions on how technology can benefit their organization. As an IT Director with many years' experience, it always concerned me that Managing Directors, Finance Directors and CEOs make decisions involving hundreds of thousands of pounds, based on complete ignorance while IT people make purchasing decisions based on pure whim or what was 'cool' at the time.

Many managers do not have time to delve deep into the mysteries of IT but need to know enough to make informed decisions or at least to be able to ask the right questions. This book is designed to take you (briefly) through the hard facts of IT such as hardware, software and networking, through what the Internet and e-commerce are, to the softer issues of developing an IT strategy from a business plan. My aim is for the book to bridge the gap between, '*those who understand what they do not manage, and those who manage what they do not understand*'. It's the same rationale for doing an MBA so that managers can talk to people in different disciplines in their language. The benefit is that they will be able to communicate more effectively with their IT people and grasp the impact that technology can have on a business.

The book is written in self-contained sections and in a light, easily digested manner, for all of us whose time is precious!

How people see information technology and why *you* need to manage it

Computers are present in practically every part of our business lives. Gone are the days where you could sit in an office and if you needed some information you would call a techie who might or might not deliver the information you required in the correct format and in time. Of course you still need the technical guys but now you, as a manager, need to understand where in your business IT can work for you and how best to implement it. Managing IT is *not* straightforward because we have a problem in our business environment. As the quote suggests, business people do not always understand IT and IT people do not always understand business. This is hardly surprising. You as a business manager have your hands full doing the day job. IT is also one of the reasons you are so busy. Gone are the days when you sent out a letter to a client, taking two or three days to reach her, then a reply took another three days to come back. Instant communications from anywhere at anytime mean that office workers get through a much greater volume of work than their grandparents did. Either our forebears were very lazy or things have changed...

Therefore there is a gap between business and IT into which our business performance falls. Let me put the following multiple choice question to you.

How do you see your IT Department?

A As colleagues with whom you regularly and formally discuss department plans and how, within the framework of an overall IT strategy, information developments can drive the organization forward and create competitive advantage for the company. ☐

B As the guys who arrive when something goes wrong with your PC. ☐

C As the guys who *don't* arrive when something goes wrong with your PC. ☐

If your answer is not A you really need to read on. By the way, if your answer is A congratulations and you're excused any further classes but read on – you might enjoy it anyway!

On the subject of Information Technology, people fall into a number of camps.

The first category consists of those who wear their ignorance as a badge of pride and hide behind an, 'Oh I don't dirty my hands with that stuff, it's all gobbledegook', attitude. They're not the people you want running a company in the twenty-first century.

Our second group is scared of IT, realizing they need to know about it but overawed by the presumed complexity and not knowing where to start. This leaves them exposed to unscrupulous salesmen who may encourage them to buy expensive but useless solutions. Training is required and they need a sympathetic teacher.

Next we find the techies, those who revere IT, seeing it as the answer to all problems and enjoying esoteric arguments about the latest firewall technology. They create disciples in each department who buy expensive bits of kit because it's 'cool', with no regard for any central strategy. Before you know where you are money is haemorrhaging from every area of the company. Train them on what the business does and teach them that IT is the servant, not the master.

Finally, a select few see IT for the powerful business tool that it is. Understanding and using it relevantly to deliver competitive advantage, they create efficiencies and a better life for staff in their organizations. Often these wise folk have also discovered that focusing on the word *'Information'* in the phrase 'Information Technology' makes it clearer and more manageable. Information flows in and between companies, is filtered through the experience of staff and becomes knowledge and even wisdom! Decide where these flows are, where you want them to be and you have evolved an information strategy. The technology needed to underpin this falls into place. Alas, few companies belong in this category. Those that do are probably keeping it quiet and just getting on with their successful lives.

This book sets out to bring everyone into the last camp, bridging the gap between IT and business and making IT work for us. One day all managers will have to understand IT and all IT people will have to understand business. Those who do so will help their organizations succeed and will command high salaries. You, as a manager, need to understand IT's potential to be a powerful force for change within your organization. According to Gartner, a research group, European companies that invest wisely in IT achieve 42 per cent higher average profits over those that don't.

They concluded: '*What we are seeing is that all IT investment has to be justified on business benefit because a lot of money is being wasted.*'

Managing IT really means knowing the questions to ask and being able to construct long-, medium- and short-term information plans. By the end of this book you will be able to do just that. As far as possible I have tried to avoid jargon but the glossary at the back explains any examples where I have veered off the straight and narrow.

Welcome then to a world where you will feel in control of IT, where you can understand it and integrate it successfully into your business!

> *Only two groups of people refer to their clients as 'users' IT people and drug pushers.*
>
> Anonymous

Let's start with the good news. It's *not* all about technology. Thomas Davenport, Professor of Management Information Systems at Boston University put it very neatly when he wrote,

> *'Imagine a world obsessed with plumbing. Hundreds of magazines and books celebrate the latest advances in valves, fixtures and pipes. Party conversation is dominated by the issue of whether one brand of sink drains faster than another. Plumbing magnates are the world's richest people. Companies pay millions to ensure that pipes reach every desk, home and office. Only one plumbing related issue is overlooked – water. Is it clean and fresh? Is water even what consumers want? Are they thirsty? A similar situation exists in real life where information technology overshadows information itself.'*

Information is the critical factor and the three areas to focus on are:

- Does your company culture support the effective use of information?
- Do you manage information properly?
- Does your technology resource (including the human element) support your information needs now and for the future?

We'll be looking at these three areas later on so relax, sit back and let's start with an overview of what the technology can do.

First of all there is a light overview of hardware. Then we subject software to the same treatment. Sharing information is of course critical, so networking and communications get their moment in the sun as well. No self-respecting book on information can ignore the Internet and e-commerce and they take a bow in Chapter 5. In each of these chapters there is also a brief guide to where you can and equally importantly, cannot, save money on these elements. Then we look at how to put into place long-, medium- and short-term plans to get IT working for you. And believe me it will. There are few more satisfying things than seeing a company transformed because its managers have taken an ambitious yet level-headed approach to gaining competitive advantage from their information. At the back of the book you will find details of where you can get more information on software and hardware agreements that can save you money.

About the author

Michael Pagan guides companies through the thickets of devising an IT strategy and making it work for them. Before starting his own company four years ago, Michael had more than 18 years' experience in managing technology in the UK and globally. He has written articles for a number of business publications and also writes advertising copy.

He lives in Hertfordshire, is married and in his spare time writes (you can probably see a theme developing here) sitcom material, plays guitar and is an active member of the local drama group.

He can be emailed on: mialp@hotmail.com

Visit the website: www.thepaganconsultancy.com

if you can kick it – it's hardware

In this chapter you will learn about:

- the different types of computer
- common devices attached to personal computers
- handheld computers
- cables and the alternatives

'Those parts of the system that you can hit with a hammer are called hardware; those program instructions that you can only curse at are called software.'

Anonymous

Hardware is the stuff you can touch, kick and throw out the window when it goes wrong: all I ask is that you open the window first and make sure no one's below.

There is a wide range of **computers** ranging from mainframes to handheld devices. We'll go through them in order of which ones you are most likely to see.

Computers

Personal computer

The personal computer (PC) arrived at the end of the 1970s. Originally created by IBM, it has become the workhorse of the desktop and has spawned many varieties such as laptops and tablet computers. Essentially, they all do the same thing allowing us to create documents, crunch numbers, communicate with our colleagues and play games. Great! And they're cheap... to buy at least, but the total cost of ownership of a PC is much higher than the £500 or so you paid for the beige box or laptop on your desk...

The most important parts are:

- **CPU (Central Processing Unit):** This is the part of your computer system that houses the hard drive, floppy disk drive, CD-ROM and most importantly the processor which does the hard work of translating what you've done into computerese and back again. CPU also refers to the chip inside the PC.
- **Keyboard:** The typewriter-like keys you use to input information and commands for your computer to understand.
- **Monitor:** This is the television-type screen of the computer.
- **Mouse:** The device that allows you to point and click on various parts of the screen to perform different functions.

Before we delve into the next bit you may be asking, 'What are megabytes etc?' They are the measurements of how much you can store on your hard disk or in memory. As a guideline, one megabyte can hold roughly 50 to 60 A4 pages of text. A gigabyte is one thousand times more than this and a terabyte is a thousand times bigger again. That's it. (Possibly also used by Bill Gates' bank manager to calculate the daily interest on the great man's account.)

If you have the inclination (and a screwdriver) the main components inside a PC are:

- **Motherboard**: This is the circuitry that connects all the internal components of a computer. No, not very interesting, but very important all the same.
- **Central Processing Unit (CPU)**: The brain of the computer that takes care of all controlling and computational tasks within the machine. Intel are the main producers in this market. However, the market is hotly contested by AMD as well.
- **Hard Drive**: The hard drive is like a gigantic set of library shelves for all your software. You copy information to your hard drive and it stays there – even when you turn your computer off at night. The size of a hard drive is measured in **gigabytes**. A standard size hard drive to purchase to run most of the software on the market today would be 60 gigabytes.
- **RAM (Random Access Memory)**: Think of it like a table in a library. You get the information from the shelves (the hard disk) and spread it out on the table to work. Then you put it back when you're finished – you save it to the hard disk. The bigger this table is, the better. Often to cure the problem of a computer freezing mid-work the solution is to turn off and on. This flushes everything out of memory or clears the library table and allows you to start afresh. Be warned though, by turning off and on you will lose any information you were working on and hadn't saved. But you save regularly don't you?

Laptops and notebooks

These are portable versions of the personal computer and vary in size and crucially weight. When choosing a laptop you have to decide on how you are going to use it. If you are a frequent traveller then it has to be lightweight, but will have to shed some items such as a CD drive or perhaps the floppy drive. These can be plugged in externally but this means carrying cables around with you. List the main things you require from the computer when travelling, to give you a good idea of the machine you need. These may include the following:

- Lightweight
- E-mail and web access
- Document writing
- Creating and amending spreadsheets
- Access to the corporate database.

In this case, you need a smaller notebook computer with a wireless network card.

However, if you only intend to carry the computer home maybe twice a week and are a graphics designer or software developer who needs more processing power, then a heavier laptop will suit you fine.

In the real world these machines are becoming more powerful and there is less need to compromise when choosing a more portable computer. One aspect that needs careful consideration is battery life. This is one area that hasn't improved exponentially.

Mainframe computers

In the beginning was the mainframe and it was very large. Webopedia describes it thus: '*A very large and expensive computer capable of supporting hundreds, or even thousands, of users simultaneously*.' Used for storing massive amounts of data by the likes of banks and insurance companies and requiring its own dedicated room and people in white coats. They still exist but fortunately, we don't have to deal with them on a daily basis. IBM, Honeywell, ICL were the biggest manufacturers.

Other hardware

Printers

Printers may be directly attached to your computer or shared via a network. This is what you use to print out your information. Modern printers only go wrong when you absolutely need them not to. They come in several flavours – here are the two most important:

Inkjet printers

These are the cheapest printers on the market today and tend to be used for home and small office work. Beware – buying the printer is just the first cost. Feeding a heavy ink cartridge habit is expensive! I reckon on spending at least the cost of the printer every year on these 'consumable' items.

Laser printers

A laser printer is different from an inkjet printer in a number of ways. The toner or ink in a laser printer is dry. In an inkjet, it's wet. The print from an inkjet printer will smear if wet, but a laser-printed document will not. Over time, an inkjet printer is about **ten times** more expensive to operate than a laser printer because ink needs replenishing more frequently. If your printing volume is high, buy a laser printer. The other big difference is when you try to lift them, laser printers being much heavier.

Drives

- **Floppy disks**: The small disks that hold an equally small amount of data. They are becoming obsolete as they are replaced by...
- **CD-ROM and DVD drives**: These are must haves if you want to play music and movies on a quiet Friday afternoon. These drives can be outside or inside your computer. They revolutionized installing software – as it used to take dozens of floppy disks to install Windows, but now it comes on one DVD-ROM. These too will become obsolete as music, videos and software are all downloaded from the Internet
- **Writeable CD-ROM and DVD drives**: These let you save and retrieve large amounts of information which can then be carried elsewhere, or if you lose a laptop, can save your life!
- **Zip Drives©**: Convenient disks for doing quick backups of small to medium amounts of information. They can be internal or external to the computer.

Scanners

A scanner analyses an image (such as a photograph, printed text, or handwriting) or an object and converts it to a digital image.

External modem

An external modem is a box that connects your computer to the Internet via a telephone line. If you're used to fast Internet access in your office and you use a dial-up modem at home, you will find it *very* slow by comparison – fine for picking up emails but that's about it. A broadband modem is a digital modem used with high-speed or cable Internet service. Modems also come in credit card sizes for laptops.

Routers

These are devices which are always connected and provide broadband access to the Internet. They often include a firewall which protects you from unwanted Internet intruders.

Network server

Network servers are the powerful, robust central computers in a network. They let us access information held centrally, printers attached to the network and other services such as Internet access. If we didn't do it this way every PC would require its own printer and other hardware. Critically, centralized information can be easily duplicated so if the main computer fails and has to be replaced, information can be restored relatively quickly. Although similar to personal computers, the components in a server are designed to reduce the likelihood of failure. As businesses become more and more reliant on computers, greater reliability and ease of service and manageability is essential. Therefore the server is not where you should try to cut costs.

Handheld computers/mobile phones

In summary there are three main types of mobile device: mobile phones; personal digital assistants; mobile email devices.

Mobile phones

Firstly the humble mobile phone which lets us talk to each other from exotic locations. It has become an indispensable business tool. The surprise success story for the mobile phone is text messaging. Mobiles now provide communications, entertainment and information all in one device. The mobile is possibly in danger of becoming a jack of all trades and master of none. It is also a fashion item. Mobiles range in price from zero to multiple thousand of pounds (see www.Vertu.com).

Personal Digital Assistants

Also known as PDAs. These started out life as electronic Filofaxes® and grew from there. I don't know where I'd be without my PDA – literally – it has mapping software that tells me where I am. The latest versions are mobile phones, or is it the latest mobile phones are PDAs as well? Anyway, the next generation will also provide 'location based services' so as you saunter down the road every branch of McDonald's®, NEXT® or FCUK® will be texting you with all the buying opportunities you're strolling past. Now we know what's been missing from our lives– can't wait.

Mobile email devices

The king of this genre, for the moment at least, is the Blackberry. With email pushed to the device (rather than you having to dial in to pick it up), Internet access, diary, addresses and a phone function, it's a bit of an electronic Swiss Army knife. As you will find out later, mobile Internet access isn't as fast as we're used to at home and this makes using the web on mobile phones slightly frustrating. That said, it is adequate for the task, provided you don't want to download huge amounts of information. If you have the relevant software installed it is also possible to view and edit spreadsheets, documents, presentations and databases with a Blackberry.

Convergence

As you can see from the descriptions above there is a lot of overlap between these devices and indeed they are morphing into one machine. The technology in this area moves rapidly and the all-in-one phone, email, television, radio, MP3 player, games player and digital assistant is the inevitable end product.

Acronyms (again)

By the way, if you've been reading articles about mobile phones and like the rest of us your head hurts as 3G, GPRS, GSM, UMTS and other weird and wonderful terms pass before your eyes, you will be unable to contain yourself for the chapter on Telecommunications which explains them all in a way that doesn't need a degree in advanced Martian (see Chapter 4).

Cables

Then there are cables. These are God's revenge on us for inventing the computer. There is a rule if you have one computer, a printer and maybe a modem, you must have at least a dozen wires snaking around and about your desk making the slightest task a nightmare. Below are a sample of common cables you will encounter. If something goes wrong with your computer, it's always worth checking first to see if a cable has become loose.

- **Network cables:** One of these connects your desktop computer to the central network computer.
- **Parallel cables:** These connect your computer to a printer. They are being replaced by the following...
- **USB cables: USB** stands for **Universal Serial Bus** and it means that instead of having a different type of cable for each function there will be a 'one size fits all' solution. About time we say! It connects a printer, a modem or any other device to your computer via the USB port at the side or back of it.

There are sundry other types of cable but we don't need to dwell on them here.

Wireless

Cables in general are fighting a rearguard action and are being replaced by wireless technologies such as Bluetooth, more of which anon. And a good thing it will be when we can reclaim our desks and floors from the curse of the cable.

Flash storage devices

Known variously as USB memory sticks, USB Flash drives, they come in all sorts of odd shapes including footballs and hearts. You can have a company logo etched on them or cover them in leather if that is your thing. Whatever shape it is, this little chap plugs into the USB port on your desktop or laptop and can hold up to 4 Gigabytes of information at the time of writing. To get an idea of what this means, it's roughly equivalent to 160,000 pages of A4 text. Ten years ago, this amount of storage would only have been available on a file server and would have cost you about £5,000. The device currently has a price tag of around £45. It can be used to save digital pictures, music, video, presentations and documents. The USB storage device's great strength is its portability. If you are going out to present to a client you can leave your laptop back in the office and plug this storage device into your client's laptop.

MP3 players

This is an incredibly competitive field. These devices let you download music and video (at a price) from the Internet and store it on a device that is little bigger than a credit card. As with many things in IT the size of the device gets smaller while its capability grows. You can now carry the contents of your entire collection of CDs and DVDs in a device that just keeps shrinking. One of the benefits of this is that you can choose the tracks you want and avoid the old problem of buying albums which had three good tracks, four so-so ones and a lot of dodgy fillers.

The top dog in this area is Apple's iPod™ but hot on its heels are a host of devices from other manufacturers such as Microsoft which has just entered the market with its Zune™. Although these are primarily entertainment devices they have a bearing on our businesses. Podcasting, which entails downloading radio and television programmes to an iPod or similar, is one of the developments that changes the way in which we consume information. This also affects how we advertise as the market becomes more fragmented and traditional media are not the only channels. Podcasting may be an effective way to get your message across to potential clients and to keep existing clients informed of developments in their field.

Attention checker quiz!

1 The box that contains hard drives, floppy disk drive, CD-ROM, DVD etc. and the chip that powers your PC are known by the same three letters. Are they:

A IBM ☐
B CPU ☐
C ATM ☐
D PSU ☐

2 Random Access Memory (RAM) will keep all your information even when the PC is turned off?

A True ☐
B False ☐

3 What is the most popular make of mobile email device at the moment?

A Palm ☐
B Nokia ☐
C Blackberry ☐

4 Where should you *not* compromise quality for cost when designing a network?

A Network server ☐
B Cabling ☐
C Backup system ☐
D All of the above ☐

5 Four gigabytes of storage is roughly equivalent to how many pages of A4 text?

A 160,000 ☐
B 75,000 ☐
C 28,000 ☐

6 Which device would you use to dial up for access to the Internet?

A Router ☐
B Server ☐
C Modem ☐

the ghost in the machine – software

In this chapter you will learn about:

- where software fits into the grand scheme of things
- questions to ask before buying
- operating systems and application software
- software you will use every day
- software to protect your company's information

'Programming today is a race between software engineers striving to build bigger and better idiot-proof programs, and the Universe trying to produce bigger and better idiots. So far, the Universe is winning.'

Rich Cook

The other part of your computer system is the software. Without software your computer will just sit on the desk. Think of it like this: A video recorder is hardware and the film you rent from Blockbusters is software. Don't be surprised when you spend £500 on a computer and find out you have to invest another £300 or more on software. When you buy a new computer most of the initial software is usually supplied to you from the factory. The irritating thing is that although software is expensive it is intangible. Unlike harware, you *can't* kick it. You *can* see the code behind it if you really want but you'll wish you hadn't. I started out in IT writing and supporting software so I have a soft spot for it.

Before buying software...

So, because of development costs, software is expensive. Before dashing out and buying the latest versions ask the following questions:

- What are the business benefits of this software?
- Has a cost–benefit analysis been done? (NB: This *must* include the potential hardware upgrades needed to run the software effectively!)
- Are the people who are going to use it aware that they are getting the upgrade, have they requested it and have they been trained in it, or is there a well structured training programme for them?
- Are your IT staff trained to support it?
- Are people using the present version to its full capacity?
- If not, why are you upgrading?

If all the signs are positive and the new software will help your business achieve its objectives, before signing the cheque just bear the following in mind:

- If you are about to buy for your entire company, can you benefit from a volume purchasing agreement?
- If your organization belongs to a larger group of companies, try to co-ordinate software purchasing and upgrading to achieve volume discounts. Maybe there's an industry body that has negotiated discounts?
- Plan the upgrade or installation as you would any other project.
- NB: Do not pirate software. It's very tempting to think 'OK, we have one copy of XYZ for Windows let's just put it on all the machines in the company.' How would you like it if one person bought your product and then copied it several hundred times? The penalties can include heavy fines and in serious cases imprisonment for directors. Additionally, if you pirate software you won't have support or documentation, essential items if you ever have a problem.

For our purposes, we can break software down into two types:

- **Operating systems:** These let *the computer* do things.
- **Applications:** These let *you* do things.

Operating systems

As a computer starts you will see loads of weird stuff flash up on screen. These are instructions to the computer telling it how it is going to talk to its chums such as the keyboard, printer and CD-Drive and how it will work with other software.

If it's the operating system for a network, then it does a bit more, such as tell the main network computer how files are going to be shunted around and who has permission to do what on the network.

Most common operating systems

This is where the fighting starts. The most common operating system is **Microsoft Windows.** Now, lots of people don't like Bill Gates for many reasons but mainly because he makes so much money! But, in his defence at least Microsoft established a standard with Windows and it has got better with each version. The most recent, Vista, was launched in early 2007 (see *Teach Yourself Windows Vista*).

Another popular operating system is Linux. It is a perfectly acceptable operating system, although it's really just another version of **UNIX** which has been around since the 1970s (see *Teach Yourself Linux*).

Applications

So, now the operating system has started up, the computer is running and there is a screen full of icons. There is an air of expectation that you have to do something. So you double click on one of the icons and it kicks off an **application** such as a word processor for you to type documents. In this section we will look at the most common applications.

Integrated suites

The idea behind this is that all the different functions work together to make us more effective. For example, we can create a graph using a spreadsheet, embed it in a word processor document and when you update the spreadsheet the graph in the document changes as well. You can also put it in a presentation, email it to interested parties or publish it on your company website.

Practical example: Makes monthly reports on the same subject much easier to create – you just have to change the figures and the charts change automatically.

Word processor

This allows you to create and edit documents and puts professional publishing tools at your disposal. Word processing software has developed over the years from simple document creation and editing to complex packages that give you the ability to embed graphics, sound and video. You can write and publish professional quality documents on the Web.

Most popular word processing package: Microsoft Word (see *Teach Yourself Word 2007*).

Spreadsheet

This is software that lets you enter numbers which can then be manipulated in a wide variety of ways. Spreadsheets are extremely powerful and useful for 'what if' scenarios, for example assessing the impact of an interest rate rise on your business profitability.

Most popular spreadsheet software: Microsoft Excel (see *Teach Yourself Excel 2007*).

Presentation software

This is used to create slides to be shown to more or less willing audiences. Presentation software can be a hero or villain. It is easy to create a tedious continuum of bad graphics and slides with too many words. One of the best slide shows I ever saw was on the very unpromising subject of hard disks. The first slide was of the presenter's dog! He was a great entertainer (the presenter not the dog). No matter how many slides or how garish the graphics, if you can't present or have nothing to say it will become apparent. In other words, the software's the easy bit.

If you like living dangerously, keep changing the presentation up to the last minute. This software uses a lot of memory and bearing in mind the rule of not letting a computer know you are in a hurry, it will crash the presentation computer just as your guests enter... Don't blame the computer or the IT guys –YOU decided to change your slides...

Most popular presentation software: Microsoft PowerPoint (see *Teach Yourself PowerPoint 2007*).

Accounting software

As your company expands you may require more sophisticated software to run your accounts and payroll. Accounting software takes some of the headache out of book-keeping.

Popular accounting software: Not the M people again but Sage whose Instant Accounts software includes these functions:

- Bank and Cash Book
- Sales and Purchase Ledgers
- VAT return
- Credit Control and Customer and Supplier records.

It also links to online Internet banking. Again to get the most from the software it is worth doing a course. (See *Teach Yourself Sage Line 50.*)

Email

Ten years ago we didn't have email. How did we live without it? Now we spend a good 20 minutes each morning wading through the irrestible offers of credit cards and slimming plans to reach the two useful and relevant emails. It *is* a valuable communications tool but management of email is essential to stop it being clogged with 'spam'. And remember, it is only part of the communications at your disposal. Don't neglect face-to-face meetings – people need people.

Most common email software:

- Microsoft Outlook
- Lotus Notes
- Novell GroupWise

Web design

Here we have quite a range of products. Web design software can be simple to use and within minutes you can produce a half decent web page. Or you can use a complex tool to develop a web page with multi-media content, online purchasing of your products and connections to databases or back office systems. In the early days of the Web your site would be viewed by a computer and therefore your website could be available in just one flavour. Now it may be looked at on the screen of a mobile phone or other mobile device. This means that a one-size-fits-all policy no longer works and design software has to cope with different formats.

Prices vary from £10 per person to £1,000+ for professional design software. As always in life you get what you pay for! Apart from the basic packages web design software really needs to be in the hands of someone trained to use it, and just as importantly, trained to know how to construct a good looking, easily navigated and friendly website. Web design software packages are legion. Two examples are:

- Microsoft Front Page: Easy to use and it combines with the rest of the Microsoft family.
- Adobe's Macromedia Studio 8: Needs the sure touch of an expert but in the right hands will produce excellent websites.

Desktop Publishing (DTP) software

Originally DTP software provided the capability of pouring text into frames producing professional documents and making the creation of indices relatively easy. As word processing software has become more powerful the lines between it and desktop publishing have blurred. Microsoft has separated its products out and Publisher is its DTP offering. Others in the field are:

- Adobe PageMaker
- Corel Ventura
- QuarkXPress

Document and content management

Document and content management is a system or software program for storing and tracking documents and other content as they pass through the company. With so much material found in a multi-media format this has expanded to include video, sound, graphics and any other content within a business process. Another form of this system, Digital Asset Management, provides for the storage of images to which information can be attached. For example, if you are creating a research document for a client it can be passed from one person to another, each adding their own contribution. Different versions are tracked and information as to who made changes and on which date, is attached to the document. Digital signatures provide security and the overall workflow process can be monitored. This can be done online so that a client is kept up to date in real time. It is also valuable for new projects so that your staff can look at a previous assignment and find where relevant knowledge resides. Document management, digital asset management and workflow all have a valuable contribution to make in managing knowledge in the organization.

Groupware

This again is software that allows collaboration, combining as it does email, databases of information. Groupware allows people to create, organize, disseminate and manage business information to give access to it when and where it is needed and in a flexible format. This is information on demand. There are similarities to document or content management and all these tools have a place in managing company information.

Popular groupware includes:

- Lotus Notes
- Novell GroupWise
- Microsoft Dynamics

Internet browser

This is your window onto the World Wide Web. At one time it was difficult to get onto the Internet and even more difficult to navigate around it. Then along came the World Wide Web which civilized most of the Internet and made it practical to do business over it. Not all Internet computers are part of the Web.

Most common browsers:

- Microsoft Internet Explorer
- Mozilla Firefox
- Netscape Navigator
- Opera

Database

The more accurate term for this should be database management tools. The database itself is like a vast library shelf containing information. To make it useful you need to index it, put it in some sort of order and be able to query it on specific criteria. For example, if I have a database of 1,000 local businesses I may only want to market to those who have between 50 and 150 employees. Then I want to narrow this further by weeding out those who are branch offices. Modern database management software makes this very easy and lets you save your search so it can be refined and used again. Databases vary in size and complexity from a simple one that keeps track of your CD or wine collection to vast beasts, for instance those used by banks.

Common database management software tools:

- Oracle
- Microsoft SQL
- Sybase
- Microsoft Access

Project management

This is software that helps you keep a tight rein on projects. You create milestones to make sure the project is on time and within budget, and the program will let you know if this is not the case. One of the strengths I find with this tool is that if something slips you can immediately see what the consequences will be for the timescale and budget for the entire project. It creates charts for planning and is generally a fine bit of kit. Initially it may seem quite expensive but if it helps you bring a project in on time and budget it will pay for itself many times over and be very good value!

Most popular project management software: Once again, it's Microsoft in the lead with Microsoft Project.

Customer Relationship Management (CRM)

Now this is serious and expensive so no chewing in class and pay attention at the back!

CRM software was supposed to deliver fabulous customer service, make it easy to attract new customers and generally make the client facing side of your business a snap (no honestly – it says so in the brochure). But did it? No it didn't. According to a recent study released by the Gartner Group, '*the proportion of unsuccessful CRM projects is due to peak at 80 per cent by the middle of 2003*'. To state the obvious, this represents a staggering waste of money. In fact if my maths is even near the mark, they mean a waste of around $3 billion. OK, so the other 20 per cent must be brilliant. Well, no, not necessarily. Gartner again: '*In reality, huge and highly disruptive implementations and a cumbersome architecture made companies less, not more responsive to customers needs.*' So the lesson here is (rather like all software implementations), know *why* you are doing it, identify realistic and measurable business benefits. Make sure the software is easily customizable for your business needs and it must be rigorously project managed. If you get the feeling that '*you just need CRM because everyone else has got it,*' go away, hide in a cupboard and don't come out until the feeling has passed.

Most popular Customer Relationship Management (CRM):

- SAP
- Oracle
- PeopleSoft

Security

This is an important and growing area. Some of these threats are a nuisance, some irritating but many are dangerous for the health of your computer's systems. As the Internet has grown so has the number of scamsters, hackers and other security risks. That said the Internet is no less secure than your fax machines, phone system or the postal system. It's down to how vigilant we all are. To help with this we need the following products.

Anti-virus software

Wikipedia, that online fount of knowledge defines a virus as,

> *'A self-replicating computer program written to alter the way a computer operates, without the permission or knowledge of the user. A true virus must replicate itself, and must execute itself. The latter criteria are often met by a virus which replaces existing executable files with a virus-infected copy. While viruses can be intentionally destructive – destroying data, for example – some viruses are benign or merely annoying.'*

The viruses themselves may be merely annoying but time spent cleaning machines eats into productivity. As with their biological counterparts, computer viruses can spread rapidly. Often they use email as a mode of transport and 'breed' by automatically mailing copies of themselves to hundreds of people in the victim's address book. If we each had 100 addresses in our contacts list then in four steps 100,000,000 computers could be infected. Serious stuff then. But help is at hand in the form of anti-virus software.

Anti-virus software analyses your computer for any unusual signs – one symptom might be lines of computer code embedded within a file. The software will then warn you of the problem if you attempt to open a file that may contain harmful code. It can also check every file on your computer retrospectively for any virus that might have slipped through the net and either delete or quarantine the file in a safe area. The company that provides access to the Internet should also provide virus checking of all emails that enter and leave your network. Preventing viruses before they are active is infinitely preferable to trying to clean up all the computers in your company at a later date.

Tips on anti-virus software

- **Anti-virus software relies on checking a file with details of the latest threats and this 'virus signature file' must be updated frequently.**
- **It is advisable to install two virus checkers, especially on network servers, so that if one misses a virus the other will catch it.**

Most popular anti-virus software: Symantec's Norton Anti-Virus.

Firewall software

A firewall acts as a barrier and hides your network from the great unknown of the Internet. Although you can get onto the Web people on the Internet cannot access your computers. The problem we have nowadays is that the boundaries of our networks are extending to people using PCs at home, in branch offices and accessing our networks with other devices. This of course means that the network must be open yet we have to protect it as well. That's how important a firewall is.

Popular firewall software includes:

- Norton Personal Firewall
- McAfee Desktop Firewall 7.5

Getting the most from software

1 Before deciding on which software you are going to deploy, involve staff who are going to use the software, in helping with selection, design, and testing.

2 Make sure people are trained on the software they use. This will help get the most out of your investment and save time, money and frustration.

3 Establish a clear lifespan for software. Again this has to tie in with where the business is going. Remember upgrades must be driven by business benefits – don't be bullied into installing the latest version by the software vendors if it isn't going to bring tangible benefits to your organization.

4 Check for volume discounts. If you are in a group of companies co-ordinate buying. This will save a lot of money.

5 Make sure new software purchases are justified and will do the job. There is only one motive – profit!

Attention checker quiz!

1 Which of the following software products lets you access the Internet?

A Norton Anti-Virus ☐
B Corel Ventura ☐
C Microsoft Explorer ☐

2 When should you buy software?

A When the business needs it ☐
B When you hear that the manufacturer has a cool new product ☐
C Every six months whether you need it or not ☐

3 Which of these is not a type of software covered in this chapter?

A Operating systems ☐
B Games ☐
C Applications ☐

4 How can you make buying software more cost effective?

A By borrowing from a neighbouring company ☐
B By writing it yourself ☐
C By buying through a volume purchasing agreement ☐
D By stealing it from your retailer ☐

5 Which application would you use to file your VAT return?

A Microsoft Access ☐
B Sage Instant Accounts ☐
C Mozilla Firefox ☐

6 According to the Gartner Group, by 2003 what proportion of Customer Relationship Management projects were unsuccessful?

A 20% ☐
B 100% ☐
C 80% ☐

joining it all up – networks

In this chapter you will learn about:

- **the business benefits of a network**
- **different types of network**
- **network components**
- **getting the most from your network**

'If computers get too powerful, we can organize them into a committee – that will do them in.'

Bradley's Bromide

The benefits of networks

After tackling the heights of hardware and the depths of software, you have taken your courage in your hands and bought a computer. Or rather, in your company you now have a computer here, one there and a few knocking about elsewhere. The problem is that some of the information Keith in Accounts wants is on Sheila in Sales' computer. So a network is called for.

Networks provide the following benefits:

Improved productivity

Networks allow Keith in Accounts and Sheila in Sales to share critical files and applications at all times, increasing accuracy and efficiency. And because networks can offer a high-speed connection to the Internet, users won't waste time waiting for pages to download or print. In addition, networks enable email communication, which helps ensure that employees – whether they're in the next office or on another continent – can communicate with each other quickly and easily.

Reduced costs

Networks can greatly reduce the cost of hardware peripherals such as modems and printers by centralizing usage and sharing them among users. Printers, for example, would be very expensive if every desktop was equipped with one. There would also be additional support costs and a much higher spend on consumables like printer cartridges. In addition, you can reduce the cost of maintaining multiple modems, dial-out lines, and Internet accounts by allowing all of your users to connect to the Internet over a single high-speed connection. It is also much easier to protect and monitor one point of access to the Internet, making your company more secure.

Better protection for your information

Information is one of your company's most important assets. Networks centralize the backup of information for your organization, making the regular protection of information a routine and straightforward task. Trying to find information on personal computers scattered here and there can be impossible whereas storing information on a server or servers allows easier access for you and your staff.

Types of network

The following are the main types you will encounter.

Peer-to-peer networks

With peer-to-peer networks, there is no central server. This configuration generally has a single string of computers connected together via cabling. Each computer is an equal, or 'peer', of the others, and it can share the files and peripherals of other computers connected to the network. This very simple type of network is generally best suited for small offices with less than five users who need to share files, printers and Internet access.

While a peer-to-peer network is a low-cost, easy-to-install solution, it has some drawbacks. If one user turns off their workstation, their information or a printer attached to their computer will no longer be available for others to share. In addition, accessing data and applications from another person's workstation can cause performance problems for that user.

Client/server networks

This is the most common type of network and means that personal computers (clients) connect to a central server. Client/server networks provide more flexibility than peer-to-peer networks. A network switch connects desktop and laptop computers to your server. This dedicated server enables people to access information and share peripherals without being dependent upon other colleagues' systems. In addition, a tape backup can be installed into a dedicated server, allowing you to back up data on both the server and all workstations. Client/

server networks are typically used when there is a constant need to access large files and applications or when multiple users want to share peripherals.

Thin-client computing

Thin-client computing shifts most of the work onto the central network server. Rather than having lots of software running on your desktop computers you just have enough to connect to the server which is where all the processing happens.

Benefits:

- Less powerful desktop computers required. The desktop computer takes all its software (including its settings) from the server.
- Easy to maintain – software installations mostly take place on the central computer instead of on a physical desktop-to-desktop basis. This can ultimately lower your total cost of ownership.

Drawbacks:

- If the central computer fails you really are in trouble. At present if a central server fails staff can carry on using their desktop computers to create spreadsheets and documents. With a thin-client device there is nothing to work with.
- Although you do not have software on the desktop computers you still need licences for every person in the company to use the central applications.
- The server has to be very powerful to run the software that would normally be on a desktop computer. Therefore the server in a thin-client network is expensive.

As the price of desktop machines has plummeted the idea of thin-client networks seems to have gone out of fashion. The concept though may reappear in a different guise when software companies start selling software as a service across the Internet. Then all we will need is a web browser and we can access the applications we want when we need them. Our use of these may be 'metered' and we'll pay on something like a quarterly or monthly basis.

Network components

In its most basic form a computer network links all the desktop PCs in a company to a central computer called a server. The network server connects to a hub from which cabling, known as the **backbone**, goes to all the floors in the building. On each floor there is a junction box and the cable for that floor spreads out from this junction box. I feel a diagram coming on. This represents the central computer and one floor with a notebook computer, a printer and Internet access. You are now the proud owner of a Local Area Network or **LAN**. At the risk of upsetting Bradley and his Bromide (?) whose quote begins this chapter, I don't see networks as committees, more as think-tanks to share knowledge and best practice.

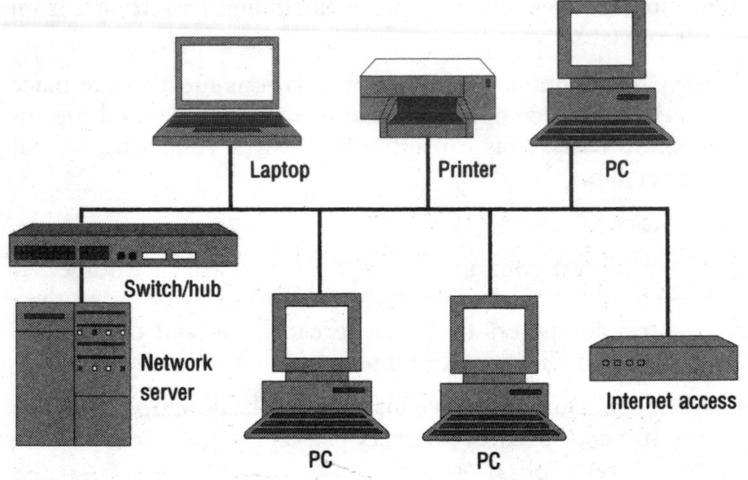

A typical network

'Never let a computer know you're in a hurry.'

Anonymous

Network configurations

How you design your network depends on how robust you want it to be, the limitations of your building and the number of computers attached to it. We will now take a look at the more popular network configurations.

Bus

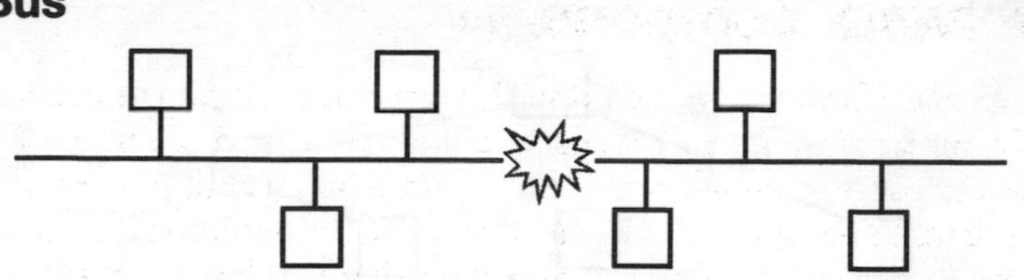

This is a line of cable with a server, desktop computers, printers and any other device you want hanging off the sides. Nice and simple but if there's a break in the cable that's it: the guys at the end will lose their connection with the network and find themselves stranded. It can also be difficult to identify where the break is.

Ring

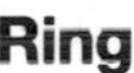

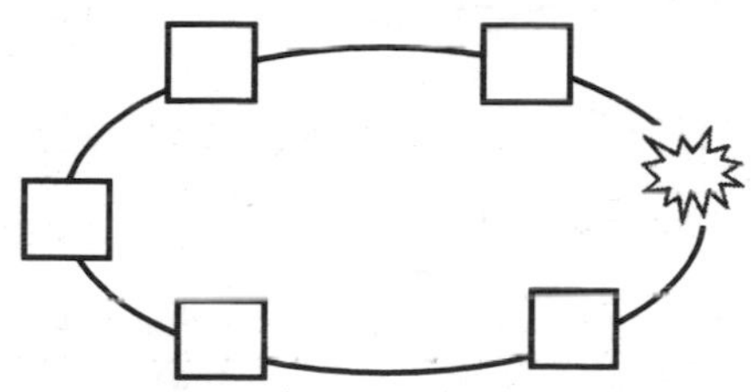

Like the bus but it joins at the ends. More resilient as traffic can usually go the other way if there's a break

Mesh

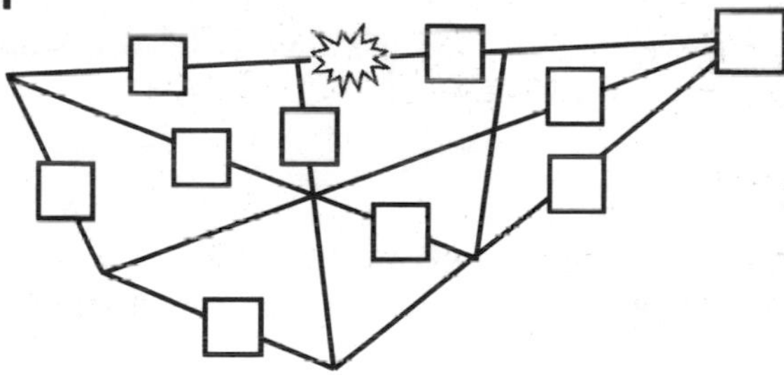

A mesh looks like a net and is highly resilient – wherever a break occurs there is usually another route for data. The Internet is a mesh, as are the public phone network and the power grid. If you need resilience then a mesh is the one for you. However, even here, if there is a problem with the server containing the particular information you need, you are not going to find it.

Tree

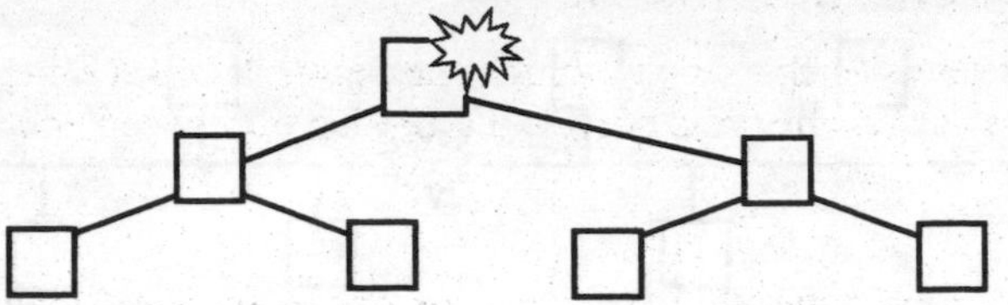

Many network systems have a tree shape. This has the main disadvantage that if the central computer goes down the entire network follows suit.

Star

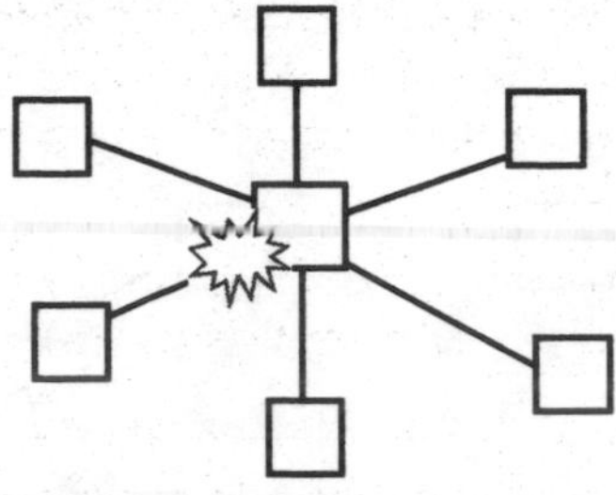

Again the disadvantage is the reliance on the central device but that applies to most networks. The way to avoid this problem is to have two servers, one of which takes over if the other fails.

Components of a network

In this section we are going to take a more detailed look at the parts making up a network.

Network server

This is the powerful central computer on the network, storing information and giving access to a range of services.

Desktop computers

These are the client computers served by the central computer. They can be ordinary desktops or laptops.

Transmission media

This refers to the way in which the network communicates with all its various bits and pieces. It's divided into wired and wireless.

Wired

For a long time we used wires or cables in our telephone and data networks. The most common cabling system is **Ethernet.** Over the years the speed at which it shunts data from one place to another has increased hugely. Just as well considering that we now blithely send chunks of information in the form of video, sound and graphics across our networks. People will talk about the pros and cons of different types of cabling but the standard is now Category 6 (Cat 6 as it's invariably known) – that's really all you need to know.

Fibre optic cabling is high speed, high capacity, high price. The following gives an idea of fibre optic's capacity:

> '*A single strand of glass fibre, thinner than a human hair, can now carry every phone call, every email, and every Web page used by every person in the world.*'

> **Hints and tips**
>
> **If you are cabling a new building do it properly to start with. When the quotation for cabling hits your desk by all means sit down and pour yourself a stiff drink. But that's *peanuts* compared with two years down the line when the network is operating at a crawl and you have to tear out old cable and start from scratch in a building where floors and ceilings will have to be 'disturbed' to do the work. If you plan this right it will be future proof for years (a millennium in computer time).**

Wireless

If you are going to be moving people and departments around a lot or you want maximum flexibility you might want to look at wireless networking. This gives us much greater flexibility in our offices. It means that staff can arrive with a laptop and work at any desk or in any room without having to search for a network point. Wireless is also the best solution if you have an old building which is listed, where space is limited or where re-cabling might be difficult and expensive. If you are in the position of having a blank sheet and are about to move into a new building it's well worth investigating wireless.

Example

I was once asked at very short notice to set up a network in a separate building but with access to the 'mother' building. Digging up roads (this was central London) was not an option... Within two days we had designed a wireless network, linked it to the main building with a wireless connection and on the Monday when the new site opened, it was up and running. You do need to be aware of security issues with a wireless network and these are covered later.

Switches and hubs

These are the junction boxes of the network through which all network traffic passes. If you have a network of more than about 50 people make sure these are up to scratch as they are key to network performance.

Networking software

Think of it like an air traffic control system for data, making sure that it doesn't collide and that it all gets to the right destination in the right order. It looks after:

- Network security by allocating who can do what on the network – after all you don't want everyone seeing the Chief Exec's bonus and saying things like, 'I think he deserves a lot more than that for all the hard work he does.'
- The flow of data – stops the bits and bytes crashing into each other and slowing things down.
- Shared services provided across the network, such as printing and email.

Most popular networking software:

- Microsoft Windows Server 2003 (or one of the earlier versions of Windows NT)
- Novell Netware
- Linux

Getting the most from networks

1 Make sure the network does what you want it to do, not what a hardware and software salesman thinks it should do. Sit down beforehand and outline what you want from it in business terms. Then and only then, start planning the technical side. That way you control costs and get what you want.

2 Make sure new networking software purchases are justified and will do the job. There is only one motive – profit! If this isn't the case then you're Enron.

3 Make sure your IT staff are trained on the networking software and monitoring tools. If you lose your network you cannot work. That's it. Now this may be no big deal some of the time but what if it's a month end? All your information, emails and the Internet are inaccessible. Using monitoring software will alert your IT team to problems before they become disasters. By the way, while the network's down, re-learn a lost skill – human contact. Get on the phone and talk to your clients or go and see them.

4 Make sure the network server is backed up every day and that a backup is regularly and frequently taken off site to a secure location.

5 If you can afford it, duplicate servers that are critical to the organization. This means that the two servers constantly update each other's information and if one fails the other takes over.

Next step

So you now have a decent network, everyone in your company is exchanging information like billy-oh and scarce or expensive resources such as colour printers are being efficiently shared. You can sit back, relax and marvel at your own brilliance. Not on your life! You may have sorted out *your* little patch but there's a big world out there. We're now going to broaden our horizons and look at Wide Area Networks.

Go west young WAN!

If you have other offices it may be useful to communicate with those locations. You need a **Wide Area Network** or **WAN**. This connects two or more corporate networks together allowing sharing of information without worrying about time or distance. Think of it like this: If your LAN is a village then a **WAN** is a country. All the information in your organization no matter where it is on the map is yours for the asking (if you have permission of course). For example you know that your Los Angeles office has had a major steel manufacturer as a client for the last five years. You are about to approach a steel company to pitch for their business. Probably worth a quick email to LA? Even better why not look directly at the presentation they did when pitching for their client's business? You can then hold a videoconference over the network and speak to the director who deals with the client while she talks you through the presentation they gave and rehearses you for the big day. Phew! Now a caveat: WANs are not to be gone into lightly. They need constant love and attention (this usually translates into money) to keep them at their peak.

Security

At this point people usually say something like: 'But if all these computers are connected together whether in a LAN or WAN, surely Keith in Accounts (perhaps in Belgium although I agree it's not a likely Belgian name) can see Sheila in Sales' figures?' Only if you want him to. Your IT team can set permissions as tightly or as loosely as you want, right down to giving Keith access to just one file.

Networks give you a lot more security than you would have if Keith was copying info onto a floppy and posting it to Sheila.

Example

I was listening to a Finance Director once raising this very issue and getting rather excited about security. Slightly later I visited the photocopier where the very same Finance Director had left his fellow Directors' salary details. All I'm saying is that security can be as tight as you need it to be using the tools of a network but it's usually the human element that messes up.

Summary

Features of a network are:

- Information is stored on a central computer and everyone can be given access to it.
- Expensive items like printers are shared among a number of people.
- Services such as the Internet or access to a database can be delivered to everyone in the company.

Benefits of a network:

- Time is saved by people sharing information more effectively.
- Money Is saved by sharing resources such as printers.
- Communication within the organization is improved through the use of tools for example email and instant messaging.
- Networks can be joined together to share information across companies, countries and continents.

Attention checker quiz!

1 Which is the most robust type of network?

A Mesh ☐
B Star ☐
C Ring ☐

2 What is the central computer in a network called?

A Peripheral ☐
B Router ☐
C Server ☐

3 What do you use to protect a network from illegal access?

A Virus checker ☐
B Firewall ☐
C Backup ☐

4 Which of the following can be accessed via a network?

A Colour printer ☐
B Fax service ☐
C Central databases ☐
D All of the above ☐

5 In general, which type of network would best suit a small office with only four computers, one printer and a limited budget?

A Peer-to-peer ☐
B Client/server ☐
C Thin-client ☐

6 Which method offers most security for sharing a confidential report?

A Copy onto a CD or disk and sending by post ☐
B Print, photocopy and distribute in the internal mail ☐
C Share via a network ☐

04 telecommunications

In this chapter you will learn about:

- **the different types of telecommunications**
- **the business benefits of telecommunications**
- **telecommuting – the pros and cons**

Background

Early computers were used for transaction processing in banks and other large organizations. Then after the revolution caused by the personal computer and with the introduction of company networks they became tools for sharing information. Then the Internet came along and made it easy to communicate with clients, partner companies and the world in general. Information that had been isolated in pockets here and there had escaped from its straitjacket and was now everywhere. When we come into the office after a holiday and discover 500+ emails or look at some of the information online, especially blogs, it's natural to feel maybe isolation wasn't such a bad thing after all...

If you think all this information must be clogging up the Internet and all the data highways that span the globe, don't worry! During the 1990s companies spent fortunes putting fibre optics into the ground. So much so that there was a huge glut and much of the fibre is still unused or 'unlit' as they say.

Remember the quote from the chapter on networking: '*A single strand of glass fibre, thinner than a human hair, can now carry every phone call, every email, and every Web page used by every person in the world.*'

Let's just think about that for a second. Combined with the commercial capacity of the Web that is staggering. If anyone says to you again, 'Will the Web change our way of working?' make them write out the quote above 100 times.

Communications

First of all there is the ordeal by acronym. Be grateful though, you might have been one of those companies who spent *billions* of dollars on buying licences for their 3G (third generation) services only to discover the next big thing in mobile phones was text messaging and not 3G services. They are still telling themselves that one day, eventually, all of us **will** want 3G services. Perhaps, but we might not want to pay the sort of money required to cover the mobile providers' debts.

Secondly, as is the way of things by the time you read this some of the information will be out of date as speeds increase and other services are offered to tempt you online. However, the following provides a broad outline.

VPN

This translates rather snappily into Virtual Private Network. A VPN connects your office to another one across the Internet without your information being visible to anyone else and therefore it is secure. Think of it like a private tunnel between you and your other office(s) through which your information can flow safely.

Broadband

Broadband refers to any service that provides fast Internet access and in effect is anything faster than dial up. The thing to remember is that like cars the faster it is the more you pay. When the Internet first appeared we accessed it via modems which allowed our computers to dial others. This was painfully slow and hampered public acceptance of the Internet. To get very fast (indeed effective) access to the Internet you had to spend a small fortune on a high-speed connection. Then some bright spark discovered a way of transmitting information over ordinary phone lines at high speed and commercial broadband was born.

DSL (Digital Subscriber Line)

There are two flavours of this: Asymmetric Digital Subscriber Line (ADSL) and Symmetric Digital Subscriber Line (SDSL). The world and its mother will have been trying to sell you this over the last couple of years. Trouble is, it's not available everywhere yet but coverage is improving rapidly. This technology uses a special modem but works over traditional phone lines – you need to connect each time you switch on your computer. The main providers are the usual suspects – BT, Orange, NTL, AOL – and some more unusual ones such as supermarkets. However in the UK they all rely on BT for the wires to carry their service.

ADSL

The word 'asymmetric' gives the game away on this one. It means that although you can get material from the Internet at one speed, sending material to the Internet is considerably slower. It's a bit like building a motorway with four lanes in one direction and one in the other. ADSL is fine for most domestic applications. However, if you have a commercial website to which you want to transfer video or other large capacity files, then bear in mind this may take some time. If you need a bit more oomph then it's time to look at...

SDSL

And of course here the key word is 'symmetric'. The motorway has four lanes in both directions and you get the same speed of transfer to and from the Internet. SDSL is recommended for companies who host their own Internet server, send large files, connect their offices with a VPN or run heavy duty business applications across the Web such as accounting software or e-commerce.

Cable broadband

Such as ntl:home. Unsurprisingly, cable uses fibre optic cable. It requires no dial-up and provides high speed access to the Internet.

ISDN

Integrated Services Digital Network uses digital phone lines and connects quickly, sending data at 64Kbps or 128Kbps. It is slow compared to ADSL and SDSL, but it was the start of the broadband revolution and made accessing the Web a more pleasant experience.

Dial-up modem

This involves dialing one modem from another to connect to the Web. Many people still use this at home. You dial-up through your phone line and the data is sent at a maximum speed of 56Kbps (kilobits per second). Painfully, maddeningly slow.

How useful is broadband?

Very. Broadband has made access to the Internet much faster and using all the services and functions out there a more pleasant experience. As a business if you have a branch office that needs to connect to your main network, ADSL (or SDSL if you can afford it) is the way to go.

Example

A small video production company in Central London was able to dramatically cut its cost of doing business with major clients by installing SDSL. These reductions were passed on to clients and they won more business on the back of improved service and keen pricing. The system paid for itself within a year.

Business benefits

Cost-effective way of connecting:

- branch offices
- remote staff
- home workers
- office staff to online systems.

Mobile phones

I'm sure we all vividly remember the days when we'd be sitting on trains bursting to shout at people, 'I'm on the train!' but couldn't. Then thankfully along came the mobile, evolving rapidly from heavy and unusable to slim and losable. The mobile is evolving into a complete entertainment centre with video, music etc. but still we use it mainly to tell loved ones we're on the train. The mobile is evolving through the following standards.

3G

Third generation (3G) mobile phones will (in theory) provide services like:

- Multimedia (voice, data, video, and remote control – you will be able to call your fridge and get it to order groceries).
- The services will work on all sorts of devices (cellular telephone, email, paging, fax, videoconferencing, and Web browsing).
- Broad bandwidth and high speed.
- It will work throughout Europe, Japan, and North America (but they're now fighting like dogs in a sack over standards).

3G was expected to reach maturity between the years 2003 and 2005. Watch this space.

Proponents of 3G technology promise that it will 'keep people connected at all times and in all places.' But how much will we actually be willing to pay for it? That is literally the 22 billion dollar question which mobile airtime providers have to earn to recover their investment in 3G licences. In reality the jury is out on 3G and it may be skipped in favour of 4G which will be true wireless broadband.

GPRS

Stands for General Packet Radio Services and is a service that promises fast(ish) continuous connection to the Internet for mobile phone and computer users. In theory the higher data rates allow users to take part in activities such as videoconferencing and interacting with multimedia websites and similar. In practice GPRS is based on Global System for Mobile (GSM) communication.

GSM

GSM (Global System for Mobile communication) is a digital mobile telephone system that is widely used in Europe and other parts of the world. The present standard for mobile phones, GSM is the de facto wireless telephone standard in Europe. It has over 120 million users worldwide and is available in 120 countries (according to the GSM MoU Association). Since many GSM network operators have roaming agreements with foreign operators, the big benefit is that users can often continue to use their mobile phones when they travel to other countries.

One of the issues about trying to use a mobile phone for Internet access is that while it's relatively fast compared, say, with using a phone to do the same thing five years ago, when put up against most people's home broadband it is frustratingly slow. This problem will remain until wireless access reaches broadband speeds (see WiMax below).

Bluetooth

Apparently Harald Bluetooth was a Danish king. Bluetooth is a computing and telecommunications industry specification that describes how mobile phones, computers, and personal digital assistants (PDAs) such as the Palm Pilot or Blackberry, can easily connect with each other and computers using a short-range wireless connection. Using this technology, people with mobile phones, pagers, and personal digital assistants will be able to buy a three-in-one phone that can double as a portable phone at home or in the office, get quickly synchronized with information in a desktop or notebook computer, send or receive a fax and, in general, have all mobile and fixed computer devices totally coordinated. Bluetooth works off a low-cost transceiver chip in each device. The transceiver transmits and receives with some variation of speed in different countries. In addition to data, up to three voice channels are available. Now you know.

Business benefit: Reduces the cost of connecting different devices such as PCs and printers by removing the need for cables. Again it gives greater flexibility to offices especially those where space is at a premium.

WiMax

WiMax refers to wireless web access at broadband or near broadband speed for homes and businesses and also mobile WiMax which offers the same performance for mobile devices. The WiMax Forum which governs the standard and should know about these things, describes WiMax as *'a standards-based technology enabling the delivery of last mile wireless broadband access as an alternative to cable and DSL'*. Just to clarify, 'last mile' is the bit between our homes and the nearest exchange. It also notes that areas of low population density and flat terrain are particularly suited to WiMax and its range. When WiMax comes into general use it will transform our mobile devices and provide broadband speeds wirelessly.

Business benefit: If any members of your workforce are mobile this will really set them free from the office.

WiFi

WiFi is short for 'wireless fidelity' and is the popular term for a high-frequency **wireless local area network** (WLAN). WiFi technology is rapidly catching on in many companies as an alternative to the traditional cabled network. It has also become commonplace for home networks.

Business benefit: In companies it gives flexibility when moving desks during those frequent periods of nomadic activity that we all indulge in. In the past when for some mysterious reason it seemed a great idea to move the finance department two floors down it was something of a major and expensive task to make sure there was adequate cabling for the new residents. If wireless is installed it's just a matter of moving the computers of those affected. (In theory really all you have to do is move the staff members since they should be able to log in at any computer on the network and access the same services from anywhere in the building. Alas people do take their PCs personally, especially if they have furnished them with three photos of their kids, a woolly troll and several stickers with rude slogans on them.)

A wireless network may also be essential if your company happens to be in an old building where you are constrained by space or planning permission.

Security

Unless properly protected, a wireless network can be open to access from the outside by unauthorized users, some of whom may have used the access as a free Internet connection. You could therefore find that although you only have 35 staff, 112 people are using your network. This does not help performance or the security of your information. When you install a wireless network add security safeguards to ring-fence it from the outside. To protect your wireless network properly the least you should do is:

- install a firewall to isolate your network from the outside world
- scramble (encrypt) data travelling across the network
- have secure and unique logins for all staff (and make sure their password isn't 'password'!).

Home working/telecommuting

The combination of all the above technologies has many benefits and offers more flexible ways of working. At the beginning of the twenty-first century it is worth asking why we insist on still behaving like Victorians and travelling into offices in city centres every day. Stop for a moment, itemize what you do during an average day. Do you have to actually be in that geographic location? Since a large number of us are now 'knowledge workers', we require a phone to contact clients and colleagues and a computer to email, develop presentations, create spreadsheets and write documents. Home working or telecommuting may not be for everyone but if you set policies then it can go a long way to improving morale, saving the environment and helping the bottom line. If a proportion of your workforce is out of the office, whether home working or on the road, you don't need the same number of seats as in a traditional Victorian command and control office. You can provide 'hot-desking' where staff do not have a fixed desk but use any free desk available.

Telecommuting provides the following benefits:

- it stops the waste of time spent commuting
- it gives you back roughly two hours of your day
- it provides a better quality of life
- it reduces pollution by cutting the number of cars on the road
- it reduces rent by cutting the floor space required for employees
- it gives you built-in disaster recovery – if there is a problem your staff can work from home rather than temporary and possibly expensive premises.

So what's not to like?

- it reduces social interaction (although frankly since much of that is standing at the water cooler discussion last night's football/soap/latest boy or girlfriend it may not be a huge loss).
- we can't keep an eye on staff. Ah! Now that's closer to the truth. The question then arises if you can't trust your staff why exactly did you employ them?

With some thought, a blend of the communications outlined above and a few ground rules, home working can bring tangible benefits to the company and the employees. Once you have these in place all you have to do is hand out the pinstriped dressing gowns!

Attention checker quiz!

1 Which of the following is a way to connect one office to another securely using the Internet?

A ISDN – Integrated Services Digital Network ☐
B VPN – Virtual Private Network ☐
C DSL – Digital Subscriber Line ☐

2 What is the main communication system for broadband Internet access?

A ISDN ☐
B GPRS - General Packet Radio Services ☐
C ADSL - Asymmetric Digital Subscriber Line ☐

3 One business benefit of broadband is?

A Faster internal company networks ☐
B Better access to services such as printing ☐
C Good connections for remote staff or home workers ☐

4 Which technology will provide wireless access to the Internet at broadband speeds?

A WiFi ☐
B WiMax ☐
C Dial up ☐

5 Harald Bluetooth was?

A The first man to use a mobile phone ☐
B A mobile phone engineer ☐
C A tenth-century Danish king ☐

6 Which is the fastest data communications standard for mobile phones?

A GPRS ☐
B GSM ☐
C 3G ☐

05 life, the internet and everything

In this chapter you will learn about:

- the history of the Internet
- business benfits of the Internet
- e-commerce
- how e-commerce can work for your business

'On the Internet, nobody knows you're a dog.'
Peter Steiner, cartoon in *The New Yorker*, July 1993

'We've heard that a million monkeys at a million keyboards could produce the complete works of Shakespeare; now, thanks to the Internet, we know that is not true.'
Robert Wilensky, professor of computer science at UC Berkeley

A brief history of the Internet

Where do you start? Rather like coming across an elephant in the dark it depends which part you bump into first. Most of us now have email accounts that rely on the Internet, some download music to their iPod via the Web while others think everyone else should be given access via the Internet, to their most profound thoughts and the exciting daily events of their lives through blogs. The Internet is at once:

- a global broadcast medium
- a way of publishing information to a potentially worldwide audience
- a means for individuals and their computers to collaborate wherever they are.

Like many things weird and wonderful, the Internet began life in the 1960s partly as a result of a study which observed that larger computer networks between different geographic locales were vulnerable to all kinds of interruptions. Therefore a robust mesh design was proposed, built and evolved into the Internet which guaranteed that if one computer was unavailable communications would go via another route. So far so good. But the original Net was a wild and woolly place used only by academics and military personnel. It had text-only content and for the average person without a degree in computer science, it was forbiddingly difficult to use. That all changed when Tim Berners-Lee, a British scientist at CERN in Switzerland, invented a way of viewing and sharing global information of all sorts, not just text. In effect he invented the first browser – the software used to view the Internet. This more manageable, humane version of the Internet is called the World Wide Web – hence the www that begins all web addresses. The Internet is now a mix of fixed line, wireless and satellite communications. It is not owned by any government or company but the technology standards which underpin it are coordinated by a body called ICANN – Internet Corporation For Assigned Names and Numbers since you ask. To differentiate between the Internet and the World Wide Web look at them this way:

- the Internet is a global collection of connected computer networks
- the World Wide Web is a collection of linked resources consisting of documents, video, sound etc. and rcsiding on computers accessed via the Internet

Business benefits of the Internet

The Internet gives companies the ability to communicate with their customers, suppliers and partners at low cost and with globally recognized standards. For example if you are running a small business and are on holiday you can keep in touch with your office and check email by:

- carrying a mobile email device such as a Blackberry
- visiting a local Internet café
- carrying a laptop with wireless access
- using your hotel's own Internet access.

The Internet provides:

- easy online ordering for your customers
- order tracking
- recognition of purchasing patterns
- automated reply to queries.

Components of the Internet

This section looks at the way information is transferred on the Internet.

Communication between individuals and groups

Electronic mail

Email lets us communicate with individuals and groups sending text, but increasingly attaching video or sound as well. It has made communication instant which can be a double-edged sword. It has also led to the curse of spam and although we are getting better at blocking it the spammers seem to be keeping ahead of the game. If you wish to advertise using email make sure the people receiving the email have agreed to it by 'opting in'. This can be done by having a contact form on your website which specifically asks visitors if they wish to receive emails from your company.

Online forums

These cover every topic under the sun and are discussion groups where people with widely varying degrees of expertise can wax lyrical on their favourite subject. Used sensitively they can attract potential clients. Don't blatantly advertise or you will be banned from the forum. Instead, where relevant provide information that other participants require and let them gradually come to see you as a reliable source of information.

Blogs

Most blogs are written and read by people with too much time on their hands. If they want to exchange the minutiae of everyday life with everyone else, fine. Just don't ask me to have to read it.

Transferring information

- **Napster:** The site originally let people swap music online for free. It has now been legalized and charges for downloads.
- **File Transfer Protocol (FTP)** is a *'language'* which allows computers to send files over the Internet.

Searching for information

- **FAQs:** ordinary text files of Frequently Asked Questions.
- **Google:** first a search engine and now much more, a 'portal'

or entry point to the Internet, supplying email and storage as well as powerful search tools.

- **Yahoo!**: one of the early directories that told you where information was on the Internet, now a search engine/portal competing with the likes of Google.

Organizing information

- **Wikipedia**: online encyclopaedia which allows contributors to add information about any subject on its site.
- **Autonomy**: search software that finds information whether it is text, video or tucked away in a foreign language newspaper. Powerful but expensive – the BBC's website is powered by Autonomy.

What is e-commerce?

> *'When I took office, only high energy physicists had ever heard of what is called the Worldwide Web... Now even my cat has its own page.'*
>
> President Bill Clinton

Electronic commerce or 'e-commerce' is the use of the Internet and World Wide Web for business transactions.

It's surprising looking back from our perspective to realize that the Internet has only been around in a commercially useable form for roughly 12 years. How did we manage before this? And did e-commerce exist before this? A brief glance at earlier versions of e-commerce highlights just how the Internet has made business-to-business (B2B) and business-to-consumer (B2C) transactions much easier and cheaper.

In an earlier incarnation e-commerce took the form of **Electronic Data Interchange** or **EDI**. EDI was a computer-to-computer based business transaction system. Major corporations such as Wal-Mart and Toyota used EDI between themselves and their suppliers to make their supply chain more efficient. Toyota especially with its 'just in time' method of working where components were delivered at the moment they were needed and no earlier, was able to reduce its inventories of parts. This gave it competitive advantage, reduced costs and set the scene for allowing customers more flexibility of choice.

Because of the specialized nature and the high cost of such systems these were not available to consumers and were solely business-to-business. Often EDI systems were designed just for that particular company and any new supplier would have to install software and hardware that might not be possible to use with any other client.

Not only was the actual software that powered the system expensive but as there was no openly available communications network, companies had to install point-to-point lines which were expensive.

Example: American Airlines SABRE system

American Airlines initiated the SABRE system in the 1960s for its own employees to schedule seats on the airline's flights. As it evolved SABRE was rolled out to travel agents who could book clients online and reduce the time taken for such transactions. In the late 1970s American Airlines extended it further by offering SABRE to their competitors and received a fee for each seat sold.

SABRE was developed further encompassing such functions as revenue management, pricing, flight scheduling, cargo, flight operations and crew scheduling.

You're probably getting the message that EDI was eye-poppingly expensive and gave larger retailers and manufacturers a great deal of power over their suppliers. Then along came the Internet...

How the Internet changes the business landscape

New business models can erupt from anywhere so analysing the competitive environment has become more difficult since the advent of the Web. For example, who would have imagined that a service started by two students in a bedroom would be sold 18 months later for $1.83 billion. But that's exactly what happened to YouTube, the video site which was bought in October 2006 by Google.

How e-commerce can work for your business

The Internet can fundamentally change the way in which we do business. If you are prepared for this it can deliver enhanced profit margins and lower transaction costs at the same time.

Example: Dell Computer Corporation

Dell was a prime example of doing business on the Web when it started selling computers direct to the customer removing the middle man. It slashed costs from its supply chain by giving customers the power to design the computer they wanted, adding components they required then ordering and paying online. Once the order was confirmed a requisition was sent electronically of course, to the component maker (Dell insisted their suppliers have a factory close to the main assembly plant to reduce the risk of interruption to supplies).

Business benefits to Dell:

- They stripped out cost from their assembly line.
- They minimized the cost of processing orders.
- They pushed the risk of holding inventory onto their suppliers.
- They were able to offer new components, such as the latest processors, from the day they were available rather than having to work through old inventory.

Benefits to customers:

- They got the computers they wanted.
- The cost reductions were passed on to them and Dell computers were significantly cheaper than the alternatives.
- They were able to track their orders online.

Competitors were unable to follow Dell's lead because they had established distribution channels which could not be easily dismantled.

Ask the right questions

Once again don't let someone else tell you that you need to be involved in e-commerce if you are not sure it's right for you. You know your business better than anyone. Check your competitors: Are they using e-commerce? If not do they know something you don't or are they missing a trick?

Be realistic: there may be some areas of your business where you can use the Internet and others where it will be of no use whatsoever. Build a compelling business case first. Set out very clearly what you want to achieve from the use of e-commerce and look at the pros and cons of each point. Maybe something along the lines of:

- Increase profit margin by reducing the costs of communications with suppliers and clients.
  - If possible take an average client and assess how much you spend on phone and fax with them per year. (Bear in mind it may also have an impact on the client.)
  - Can this be reduced if you used email?
  - Might this have a detrimental effect on client relations?
- Better client service.
  - Keeping your clients better informed by giving them secure access to their latest project or letting them query invoices online may tie them closer to you.
- Reduced costs of reaching new and existing clients.
  - Creating a monthly newsletter can be an effective way of keeping in touch with existing clients and making your company known to potential new ones.
  - If you are a retailer creating an online shop window you will be competing with a huge number of companies across the world.
  - Rather than market in the traditional way, creating an online community for devotees to discuss products similar to yours and swap experiences can result in prospective customers going to your site instinctively and staying to buy your product.
- Access to a much wider range of clients.

How much change can you handle?

You have to weigh up the impact on your existing business model. It may well be that this is defunct and a wholesale reinvention of your business is necessary. This level of change will be painful and disruptive but may bring great rewards.

Analyse to what extent you think you wish to be involved in e-commerce. It can range from a simple one-page website advertising your company right up to a full order fulfilment service linked to your back office systems. Clearly the cost of these two visions of e-commerce is very different. However, it is possible to start off modestly and scale up as you, your employees and clients become familiar with using e-commerce tools. Bear in mind though that:

- There is a relatively low cost of entry into e-commerce.
- A fast return on investment is possible.
- Because the systems used are 'open' (not restricted to one supplier) there is great flexibility resulting in lower costs.

There are other issues that you will have to consider. The global nature of the Web means that you are potentially opening your business up to the entire world. The following checklist is only a guide and none of these, if they turn up a negative, should stop you considering e-commerce in general as a business tool:

Clients

- **Do your clients want to use the Internet to do business with you?** ☐
  - **Do they have security concerns? (This is a key area. If your clients are involved in the financial, pharmaceutical, defence or other industry which has sensitivity regarding security, make sure their concerns are addressed.)** ☐
  - **Have you security in place to protect financial or commercially sensitive information sent over the Internet?** ☐

Legislation

- **Are you providing something for which different countries have different laws? (A recent example of** ☐

this is the way online gambling has been badly affected after the US government legislated against it.)

Cultural

- Do other cultures use your product in the same way as existing clients? ☐
- Might it be offensive to them? ☐
- Is there already a dominant supplier in the market? ☐

Capability of your workforce

- Do your staff understand how the new business model will work? ☐
- Are they ready for potentially rapid growth in demand for your product or service? ☐

Back office

- Can your accounting, ordering and invoicing software cope with a sudden increase in orders? ☐

Infrastructure

- Have you got the distribution channels in place for your product or service? ☐
- Is there an existing distributor you could use? ☐

Can you handle it?

- If you start taking orders on an Internet site can you fulfil those orders within the (ever more demanding) timeframe required by your (ever more demanding) clients? ☐

Security

- This is critical. Your clients need to know that they can order and pay for products on your e-commerce site without the risk of fraud. Make sure your supplier has the highest security level possible. ☐

To answer the questions raised in this section's headers, e-commerce can work for you in the following ways:

1 It can lower the cost of reaching your clients, suppliers and partner companies.

2 In business we are all seeking to remove any obstacle between the client and our product or service. E-commerce helps us quite a way towards this Utopian vision. If all a client has to do is login securely to your site, browse for a product, click on it and drop it into an online shopping cart it makes the whole experience practically effortless. Just think of Amazon, an online bookstore. It makes it easy to find books you want and suggests ones that you didn't know you wanted based on your previous purchases. This feature is so effective that my bank manager has banned me from using Amazon but it is a powerful marketing tool to know what your client wants before they do!

3 It can provide a customized or personalized service to clients for them to design and buy your product or service online.

4 Mass customization gives your customer control over the product that they are buying. Even car companies are discovering this and allowing customers to choose colour, interior trim, engine type and other features when ordering their vehicle, all from the convenience of their computer. So now you know what your employees are doing with Internet access!

5 It can provide a self-service element for your product or service.

6 A small telecoms company selling one manufacturer's phone systems developed a website to allow customers to order online. As the site grew clients gravitated to it as a centre of authoritative information. The driver behind the site was the simple question, 'What are our clients' biggest headaches?' and providing solutions to this became the service. The independent advice provided gave the company the impetus to start selling other systems and their business grew exponentially.

7 It can create a community of people interested in your product to the extent that they will suggest changes to its design. This is the famous 'word of mouse', where people who are interested in your product swap information about its qualities and drawbacks. Think of it as an expert focus group which can help you understand your market and customers in great detail.

8 To reduce inventory and create a just-in-time supply chain.

What your clients will expect

- Availability: Always on becomes the norm and your site must be available 24 hours a day, 365 days a year.
- Ubiquity: Just about every company now has Internet access. The assumption will be that you will have it as well.
- Global reach: Your site will be available from anywhere in the world. Therefore be prepared to expand your horizons!
- Digitization: Working out how much of the supply chain that links you to your clients and suppliers can be done electronically, and depends on your product range. If you are a manufacturer with a physical product obviously there has to be physical delivery but researching the product, ordering and payments can be digitized. The obvious example is Dell. On the other hand if you are a publisher of products that can be delivered electronically (software, music, movies, games etc.) then the entire transaction can take place online; example: Adobe.
- Multimedia: More and more we expect a richer experience when we go online. We want to see video, hear sounds and be entertained.
- Interactivity.
- Community.

How do you start?

E-commerce applications must be very closely tied in with business strategy. They can significantly change they way in which you do business. Prepare and involve your staff all the way through the project and you will succeed.

Case study: The Coffee Company

The business

Established in 1969, The Coffee Company, sells retail and wholesale coffee through their Carlisle Street store in Balaclava, Melbourne. They also roast beans on the premises. The Coffee

Company also retails a variety of herbal and fruit infusion teas, roasted nuts, dried fruits along with homeware related to the brewing and serving of coffee and teas. The business employs seven staff.

What was initiated?

The website, **www.coffeecompany.com.au**, was first developed in 1999 with modest expectations. As the customer experience

was focused on visiting the shop, Alex – the proprietor – could not imagine why people would buy products online without walking through the door! As the visitors to the website grew, more information and products were offered for sale. Customers can now view stock from the shop, research coffee, tea and related homeware and purchase via a Secure Payment Gateway. The site is also a valuable resource guide for all things coffee with an array of coffee links provided.

> **What is a secure payment gateway?**
>
> A payment system that allows customers to make secure credit card payments across a website. The system encrypts credit card details to ensure that they remain secure from hacking and subsequent fraudulent use.

Results

Over 300 orders have been received via the secure payment gateway in an 18 month period. Now, there is hardly a day goes by without an order. The Coffee Company website, complete with a secure payment gateway has developed a significant revenue source from people who either shop online because they are unable to visit the shop or research their purchase online to then come and buy later.

How the technology works

The secure payment gateway works by processing the credit card details of the customer and passing the order via email to the Coffee Company for fulfilment. The process is outlined below:

1 The customer enters their order into the site including their credit card details.

2 The order is encrypted with the credit card payment being processed by the Secure Payment Gateway.

3 At the same time, an email is sent to the Coffee Company with the customer details and the items they wish to purchase.

4 Management instructs one of the staff to gather the items and prepare them to be posted.

5 The order is delivered with the daily post by Australia Post.

Outcome

The Coffee Company website was launched in 1999 and within five years it was a significant contributing channel to the business. The contribution to revenue measured against outgoings reveal an overall return on investment of $74,400.

Costs

Both establishment and ongoing costs were relatively low with the major expense being the establishment of the website at $2,000, amortized at $400 over five years.

The human resource to update the website has been Alex's time but this is limited depending on how busy the business is. Overall, the upfront expenses came to $3,600 during 2003 with operational expenses amounting to $2,000. One expense that the Coffee Company incurred wisely was the purchase of Anti-Virus software for $200. It is important to ask your Internet Service Provider or web developer about Internet Security, firewall and antivirus software when you set up your Internet access.

Challenges

The introduction of the website has not presented any major challenges nor changed processes within the 'real world' retail store. One process that the Coffee Company has changed is the daily visits to the post office to dispatch the orders. This fulfilment of orders via Australia Post mail has been scheduled as part of the existing staff duties. The management of the Coffee Company found that the website volume is not yet large enough to warrant a dedicated staff member and given the solid return on investment is looking forward to the sales volume to grow further.

Future plans

The Coffee Company is planning on increasing the content to the website and providing even more detail about their coffee and tea products. The Coffee Company is also actively working to improve their listings on Internet search engines as a method of increasing website traffic.

Figures

(Additional revenue from e-commerce in Australian $)

Direct sales via the Internet	50,000
Indirect sales via the Internet (estimated)	100,000
Gross benefit from e-commerce	150,000
Less: Cost of goods sold	70,000
Net profit for e-commerce	80,000
Less: Up front fixed expenses	
Website and content management systems*	400
Anti-virus and security software	200
Computer software	1,000
Computer hardware including modem	2,000
Total e-commerce up front fixed expenses	3,600
Less: E-commerce operational expenses	
Domain charges (Web address)	200
Internet service provider/hosting of website	500
Technical support	100
Postage charges	600
Telecommunication charges	600
Total e-commerce operational expenses	2,000
Total e-commerce costs	5,600
Total e-commerce benefit	**74,400**

For further information go to: www.mmv.vic.gov.au/casestudies.

Attention checker quiz!

1 Who is credited with making the World Wide Web accessible and easy to navigate?

A Bill Gates ☐
B Larry Ellison ☐
C Tim Berners-Lee ☐

2 Before the Internet e-commerce existed under which snappy title?

A Electronic Consumer Transactions ☐
B Electronic Data Interchange ☐
C Electronic Commercial System ☐

3 If you wanted to send a client a routine report how would you do it?

A Email ☐
B Online forum ☐
C Blog ☐

4 The body which sets technology standards for the Internet is called?

A The UN Internet Group ☐
B Internet Corporation for Assigned Names and Numbers ☐
C Internet Alliance ☐

5 Which one of the following is *not* a search engine?

A Google ☐
B Yahoo! ☐
C Napster ☐

6 Wikipedia is which of the following?

A An online encyclopaedia ☐
B A website for new age hippies ☐
C A music download site ☐

06 starting out

In this chapter you will learn:

- **how to create a multi-disciplinary team to manage IT**
- **how to use your business plan to identify where information fits in**
- **how to assess your present IT capability**

'The starting point of all achievement is desire.'

Napoleon Hill

Where do I start?

There are many more quotes about starting and how the first step is always the most difficult etc. There is a lot of truth in this. It can seem daunting so the following table gives an overview of how we're going to go about planning and implementing a roadmap for information.

Stages of planning for information

Starting out	What do we need to do to start moving forward with information in our company?
Information vision	How do we sum up where we want to go with information?
Information architecture	What hardware and software are needed to get us where we want to be?
Long-term plan	Three years from now what do we want to have achieved through our use of information?
Medium-term plan	What do we need to do over the next 2 years to move our plan along?
Short-term plan	What do we need to do this year to move our plan along?

Why do you want to manage information resources?

We're constantly being told we live in a knowledge economy so it's quite surprising the level of ignorance that still exists! Possibly this is because we've got so much information we don't know what to do with it. It's all too easy to jump straight in and write an information plan by yourself, chuck it on a shelf and forget about it. This chapter prepares you for the road ahead where you will create an information plan that will last.

But apart from all that, what has information ever done for us?

Presumably you want your business to perform better and you recognize that IT can help you.

Managing information means getting the most out of your investment in technology and the people who oversee it. In short, you need to ensure that the right people have the right information at the right time. There is no point having vast amounts of information about your business and industry if you do not know where it is, how to reach it, it is in the wrong format or is out of date. Information must be timely, relevant, accurate and fresh. Managing information resources, when done properly, can:

- improve client relationships
- help you win new clients
- increase job satisfaction for staff
- increase staff retention thus lowering recruitment costs
- make more effective use of people's time
- increase profit margins
- reduce costs.

In the end what begins life as a rather nebulous information plan ends up as hardware and software sitting on your and your employees' desks, helping you drive the business forward.

How do you manage information resources?

Remember the plumbing and water analogy in the Introduction? To reiterate, it is **information** which is the important bit – the technology will follow. The first part of any venture is gritting your teeth and actually getting on with it. Firstly you have to prepare the ground so that you have a clear picture of how information resources in the organization will be used.

There are three stages to this preparation:

1 Create a multi-disciplinary team.
2 Identify from the business plan where information can play its part.
3 Assess your existing information capability.

1 Create a multi-disciplinary team

There is a saying that 'IT is too important to be left to IT people'. (I've also heard the same mantra about Marketing, Finance and all the other operational areas but since we're talking IT here let's focus on the IT guys.) This means no disrespect to those of us who are IT professionals but reflects the way in which IT has an impact on every function within an organization. It makes sense therefore to create a small group from across the company and beyond to examine where and how IT could benefit the business.

Make it exciting! Imagine. This is nothing less than an opportunity to transform your company's future. This group of people can imagine a future where you are using information to make your and your clients' lives better. If you can communicate this to the group from the outset then they will be enthused and will rise to the challenge. Why not take them to an inspiring place to launch the group? A local art gallery perhaps or a science museum – anywhere that gets them away from the day to day (unless of course you own an art gallery or run a science museum).

Once fired up this group acts as a technology board and a conduit for creative ideas about information. It should report to the Chief Executive and if possible the Chief Executive ought to chair meetings of this group, giving it authority, credibility and stopping it becoming a discussion group about someone's printer problems or other operational support issues. It must have a visionary remit.

For practicality's sake it should consist of no more than six people. If you are a smaller company it can be three or four in number. Although these people will have been chosen for their interest in technology, they should not be pushing the narrow interests of their own departments but forming a business and technology think tank. Their brief is to map out the information future of the company.

A typical technology board might include members drawn from IT, Marketing and Finance as well as a board level manager to give it clout. It can also be a forum where invited guests from outside the company contribute to give a wider perspective. The views of clients, suppliers and academics may bring insight and a refreshingly different perspective to the group's discussions. Finding a tame client to talk to about the strengths, weaknesses and possibilities for your use of information can be very valuable. It can also be quite enlightening how your view of what you should be doing differs from your client's...

The functions of this group are to:

- Identify where information can bring benefit to the organization.
- Scan technological developments and identify whether new technologies can benefit the organization.
- Set out long-, medium- and short-term goals for information in the company.
- Oversee the implementation of new technologies to achieve these goals.
- Ensure the organization uses existing systems effectively.

2 Identify from the business plan where information can play its part

An IT plan can only be as good as your business plan. Therefore the first port of call is your business plan which will outline general objectives. Analyse these objectives and decide what information is needed to make them happen. The more specific the objectives of your business plan, the easier it is to identify where IT can and cannot help. Our sample company (a business consultancy) wishes to fulfil the following major objectives:

- To increase revenue to £1.8 million in financial year 2007.
- Increase gross margin to 24 per cent from 18 per cent in financial year 2007.
- To improve the quality of information provided to clients during projects.
- Use initial clients to continuously improve service offerings and act as references for potential clients.

Taking each objective, identify how information can play a role in its achievement.

For example, improving customer retention could well require the development of better electronic links with customers. Or it may be that more efficient systems in house allow your staff to go out and spend time with clients thus improving customer service. In the table below we take four business objectives and outline where information can assist in achieving them. These can be as simple or as complex as you wish. Remember, of course, that there will be times when information planning is not relevant to achieving a business objective.

Business objective	Information's contribution to achieving it
To increase revenue to £1.8 million in financial year 2007.	Use learning from live and completed projects and make available online to sell new services to clients.
To increase gross margin to 24 per cent from 18 per cent in financial year 2007.	Use price checking on the Web. Where possible buy directly online from suppliers.
To improve the quality of information provided to clients during projects.	Give clients secure access to relevant information during projects.
Use initial clients to continuously improve service offerings and act as references for potential clients.	Allow clients to post comments and engage in discussions on projects via an extranet.

3 Assess your existing information capability

Why do we need to assess information resources? Information swirls through your business, some of it sticking in nooks and crannies you weren't even aware existed. It finds its way into the heads of you and your staff, gets filtered through your experience and becomes more valuable to the organization. Some of it is also *unique* to your organization. This highly valuable resource helps you win new clients and keeps existing clients very happy. Or at least it should. Yet how often do we treat information and knowledge like a waste product after a project is complete?

We need to ask the following questions:

- What information is of value?
- Are people in the company aware of it?
- Will they share it?
- Is it fresh, accurate and relevant?

These sorts of questions tell us that we need to plan how information is used. In this part we look at how to analyse a business's information capability. By doing so we can create a plan that is flexible enough to allow for changes in the economic, political, legislative and competitive environment. Much of the theory in this chapter is based on the book *Making the Invisible Visible* by Marchand, Kettinger and Rollins (Wiley, 2001) and I am indebted to them for a method which comes as close as I've seen to solving the thorny problem of measuring the value of IT to companies. It's well worth reading. In this work Marchand and colleagues identify and define the following four types of company:

1 *Self-aware winner*: Companies, divisions or business units that understand how to manage their information capabilities to improve their information orientation and to achieve superior business performance.

2 *Winner at risk*: Companies, divisions or business units that deliver good performance results at present but lack the capabilities for the future.

3 *Info-oriented laggard*: Companies, divisions or business units that understand how to improve their information capabilities but suffer from other fundamental business weaknesses.

4 *Blind and confused*: Companies, divisions or business units that have not improved information capabilities in the past and have suffered poor performance. These companies are in need of a major business change to significantly transform their information capabilities and business performance.

How do we assess information resources?

Three key measurements will tell you how good you are at using information.

1 **Information culture**: The ability of a company to provide a climate for its people to use information effectively.

2 **Information management**: The ability of a company to manage information as a valuable resource.

3 **Information technology**: The ability of a company to use technology resources effectively.

1 How does the culture of your organization support the effective use of information?

Checklist:

- How do people in the organization actively seek out and use information?
- How freely do people share information?
- How freely can mistakes be admitted and can they be discussed openly without fear of punishment?
- How freely are all employees informed about business performance?
- To what extent do staff use and trust formal information sources to provide them with honest, accurate information?
- To what extent is there effective sharing of sensitive information?

2 How does your company manage information?

Checklist:

- How do you find information such as your clients' demands for new products?
- How do you identify potential problems with suppliers?
- Do you know what information employees need so you can collect relevant information and don't subject them to information overload?

- Is it easy to access existing knowledge in the company?
- In what way is information organized for effective use?
- How is information processed into effective knowledge?
- How is information maintained so that people are using the best available?

3 How does the IT function effectively support information?

Checklist:

- To what extent are the hardware, software and telecommunications capabilities in place to support executive decision making?
- To what extent are the hardware, software and telecommunications capabilities in place to enable development of new ideas, products and services?
- How does the use of hardware, software networks and technical expertise support people within the company and your clients, suppliers and partners?
- To what extent are the hardware, software and telecommunications capabilities in place to support business operations?

Look at the results objectively. If the results of the assessment look bad, **don't panic!** If the results of the assessment look good, **don't get complacent!**

The assessment is only designed to show you the strengths and weaknesses of the way your organization uses information so you can start building from there. It is also an exercise you should do on a regular basis not just as a one off. Strategy development is a journey, not a destination. Once you've got this bit done you know where you are and can start moving forward and making IT work for you.

Beware! It's very easy to measure *IT performance* but not link it to *business performance*! For example, I know of a company where they analysed the time periods between servers having problems. One server had had **no** crashes whatsoever. On the face of it this looked like a very successful implementation of hardware. They were about to celebrate their technological prowess until someone asked 'Who uses this server and what does it do?' They then discovered it wasn't used by anyone and had been surreptitiously bought by a department for a software product that had never worked! There must be clear business performance measurements to assess the value of IT practices.

Checklist: Dos and don'ts of assessing your information capability

Do:

- **Make sure every department is represented.**
- **Look at the information objectively.**
- **Communicate the results to the whole company.**

Don't:

- **Ignore the results.**
- **Be disheartened if the results seem poor (you're way ahead of competitors who haven't even undertaken the exercise).**

Resources to help you

On my website, www.thepaganconsultancy.com, you'll find a questionnaire we've developed to help you assess which of these categories your business may be in.

The questionnaire seeks to uncover the strengths and weaknesses of your approach to information. Once it has been completed you will have three graphs that illustrate how close to or far away from, the ideal your organization is in respect of:

- How the culture of a company supports the effective use of information.
- How information is managed.
- How IT supports the use of information.

Attention checker quiz!

1 What is the purpose of a multi-disciplinary technology group?

A To decide what hardware and software to buy ☐
B To fix occasional printer problems ☐
C To steer the future of information in the company ☐

2 Where do the objectives for information come from?

A Questionnaire to all staff ☐
B Business plan ☐
C They are made up on the hoof ☐

3 The ability of a company to provide a climate for its people to use information effectively describes which of the following?

A Information culture ☐
B Information management ☐
C Information technology ☐

4 Which of the following statements comes under the heading of Information Management?

A Staff use and trust formal information sources to provide them with honest, accurate information ☐
B Hardware, software and telecommunications capabilities are in place to support executive decision making ☐
C Information is organized for effective use ☐

5 If a company understands its information capability and is sure of the future direction for information it could be described as what?

A Self-aware winner ☐
B Info-oriented laggard ☐
C Winner at risk ☐

6 The IT board should include members from which of the following departments?

A Information Technology ☐
B Finance ☐
C Management ☐
D All of the above ☐

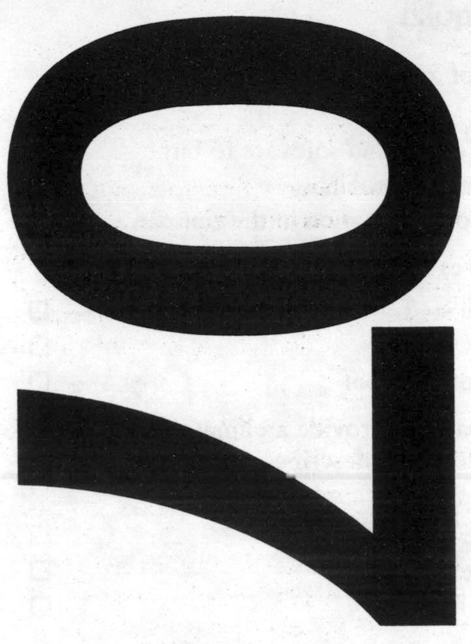

information vision and architecture

In this chapter you will learn:

- **what is an information vision**
- **how to create an information vision**
- **what an information architecture is and how to create one**

'Oh yeah, the vision thing.'

George Bush Snr

What is an Information Vision?

First of all you need a vision describing where you want to be with Information Technology over a certain timescale. Although it sounds like it, an Information Vision isn't something that happens after sitting on a mountainside in Nepal and having a mystic experience about your computer systems. Give yourself a bit of freedom on this. Don't try to do a huge amount in an unrealistically short time!

The Information Vision is a mission statement for what you want to do with information in your company. And if you hate the words 'mission statement' you're not alone as the following quote shows:

> *'You know you've got a rockin' Mission Statement when it inspires the employees to think of themselves as being involved in something much more important than their pathetic, underpaid little jobs, when they feel part of a much larger plan, something that can shape the society they live in.'*
>
> Scott Adams, *The Dilbert Principle*

But to be less cynical, mission statements and information visions are vital to planning. Imagine the following. A great artist has a vague idea about a painting; it coalesces into a vision in his head. He goes out, gets himself a few paints, brushes and a canvas. And a model of course. Before you can say 'Da Vinci Code', there's the *Mona Lisa* hanging on his wall!

By definition these statements are top level and not specific, hence the suspicion with which they are viewed.

An **Information Vision** therefore is a written expression of your ambition for information use in the organization. It is the chance to set out how information will work for you, delivering value and adding to the bottom line. This is an *ideal* view of the future that you can work towards and *not* a detailed plan on how to get there (that is dealt with later).

How to develop an Information Vision

Let me say first off, and I can't reiterate this enough, it's all about **people**, the **information** they need and **how** they use it. Technology is just the medium for getting information from the heads of your staff or external sources and sorting, storing, cataloguing and distributing it to those who need it.

Development of an IT Vision and Architecture has to be done either by or with reference to all disciplines or departments of your organization. Think of it like this: if you were sitting at your desk and someone wandered up and said, '*Hey, we're going to do things like this from now on*', you'd be really irritated that you hadn't been consulted. History holds a list of IT projects as long as my arm that have failed because people weren't consulted before major changes that radically affected their jobs were made. In fact I'd go further and say that most failed IT projects are down to a lack of consultation. Let people research, identify, test, break and retest systems before you buy them and I guarantee they will be evangelists for the new stuff and your project success rate will be close to 100 per cent. Experience shows that a small core group bringing other members of the organization in on a consultancy basis is the most effective way to work, as follows:

- The Information Group created earlier (see Chapter 6) will research and draft the Information Vision. For this task it is important they work closely as a team. Technical questions will arise and will need to be answered by IT staff. Remember though that the Information Vision is a wish list for where you want to be with information – don't get too bogged down in detail!
- The Information Group's first task is to get out and talk to people across the company and beyond so that the Information Vision reflects everybody's interests. This paves the way for providing reliable information services to all clients, whether inside or outside, the company.
- Next they need to gather all the information and sort it into the following categories:
  - technical
  - human.

- Following this they can split it under these headings for the technical parts:
  - hardware
  - operating systems software
  - application software
  - network software
  - data/information.

  And these for the human:
  - personnel
  - values and culture
  - management of systems
  - training.
- Finally, the job of the Information Group at this stage is to boil all your different ideas down to a single statement of intent that will focus you and your team on what is important. This is the information mission statement that identifies what you hope to achieve and rather like an advertising slogan, it is an essential tool for selling the idea to others. The key is to keep it tight, but consult widely. Once you've got an Information Vision together celebrate – you've achieved a major milestone in managing information for success.

Pointers and questions to ask

Start by looking perhaps three years ahead and deciding where you would like to be in terms of your use of information. This must of course be in line with the business plan for the same time period. Vision creation starts with research as to how the competitive environment will change and how the business should take advantage of this.

Some key questions are:

- What information will improve the effectiveness of people inside and outside your company?
- What information will improve your business processes and operations?

- What information will improve your ability to innovate and produce new products or services?
- What information will foster more effective decision making in management?

Keep the vision statement short – you have to be able to communicate it easily to those who will make it happen. You should end up with something like this:

> 'The organization's information resources will provide reliable, accurate, timely and relevant information to all clients inside and outside the company.'

It's very top line and now needs more detail to be added but it gives a sound platform for developing the vision. Expand this into:

- The effectiveness of all staff will be improved by access to desktop systems (both hardware and software) delivering timely, relevant, fresh and accurate information.
- All existing business support processes (e.g. order processing) will be automated to free staff time for more valuable (maybe client-facing) activities.
- Each department will be responsible for managing its own information and technology resources within a company-wide information technology framework.
- All staff will have access to the Internet for research and communication.
- Key staff will have remote access to the corporate network.
- Clients will have access to secure areas of the corporate network.
- The corporate network will be designed to cope with large volumes of data from clients, suppliers and partners.
- Management will know how to use information to make decisions and how to use all information resources effectively.

Sample Information Vision

The example below is taken from a printing company.

Information Vision

> 'Information Services will supply reliable information, data and computing services to all clients whether inside or outside the company. Information Services will support the objective of achieving a 15 per cent improvement in productivity.'

This was developed into the following:

- We will reduce the job cycle from order to delivery.
- We will increase the productivity of every person in the company.
- We will work towards zero defects in everything we do.
- We will accept jobs electronically from all customers.
- We will improve company management systems such as personnel, payroll and budgeting.

That's the statement of intent as to how information will be used in the company. Now we have to create a physical framework for this to progress – **Information Architecture.**

What is an Information Architecture?

An Information Architecture outlines how the Information Vision will be achieved through the use of technology and human resources. Consisting of hardware, software and human elements it is the framework around which future developments will be built.

Why develop an Information Architecture?

In this stage you are moving from the nebulous Information Vision into the real world of hardware and software which will be needed to make the vision happen. You've mapped out where you want to get to; now you have to decide what resources are required to get there. Just the act of designing an Information Architecture helps you build a platform for future information planning.

How to develop an Information Architecture

The Information Architecture should be designed by technology people in conjunction with business managers. For IT to really work properly it is essential to have commitment from departmental managers to moving the company forward in its use of information. We all know that departments love to 'compete' but just for once get them to co-operate. It may not be as much fun but it will improve the performance of the company! Whichever way you do it, the result will be a set of policies similar to the ones below. As it can be a lengthy list, it helps to break this activity down into technical and human elements. In addition don't try to do it all at once...

Outline of technical policy

The elements involved in the technical policy are the following:

- hardware
- operating systems software
- application software
- network software
- data/information.

These headings can be expanded into the following:

- Critical information is stored in a secure environment.
- Critical information is regularly and frequently backed up.
- The backup is taken off site to a secure location.
- Regular test restoration of information is carried out.
- The management of information must be supported by an excellent technical infrastructure.
- All staff will have access to a high performance network providing easy access to the internal and external information required for their roles.
- All critical information and systems will be available on the company network.
- Systems development will follow guidelines developed by the Information Management Group.

- All information systems in the company will be chosen from a list approved by the Information Management Group.
- The Information Management Group will maintain a list of supported word processing, spreadsheet, database, email, Internet browser and statistical analysis software.
- Departments may suggest applications for this list to the Information Management Group
- If a department buys software not on the approved list it will not be supported by the Information Services Group.
- Each department manager will be responsible for information maintained by his/her department.
- The Information Services Group will provide support for a set of hardware and operating systems approved by the Information Management Group.

Outline of human policy

The elements involved in the human policy are the following:

- personnel
- values and culture
- management of systems
- training.

These headings can be expanded into the following:

- Trained clients will be provided with a secure login and password so that they may access information stored on the company network.
- The Information Management Group will have overall responsibility for quality and cost of information required for the effective running of the company.
- The Information Management Group and the Information Services Group will have responsibility for ensuring that components of individual systems comply with the information architecture.
- The Information Management Group will develop and maintain policies related to information systems development.

- The Information Management Group will oversee and update the company's information architecture.
- The Information Management Group will set and approve budgets for information systems and architecture.
- The IT Manager will lead and support development and maintenance of a company-wide information system for the organization.
- The IT Manager will be responsible for maintaining and improving the technical infrastructure.
- The IT Manager will be responsible for long-term technical development and support of staff.
- The IT Manager will support the continuous improvement of information in the company.
- The IT Manager will be responsible for maintaining and improving existing information systems.
- The Information Services Group will be responsible for support for development of new application systems.
- The Information Services Group will be responsible for maintenance and upgrade of existing systems.
- Each manager in the company will have responsibility for the budget and planning for an information systems plan that meets his or her department's requirements.
- The IT Manager will ensure that in conjunction with him/her each department has developed its own information plan.
- Every member of staff will have at least 24 hours of IT training every year and this will form part of the appraisal and bonus scheme.

Sample Information Architecture

Technology component

- The entire information creation process must be supported by an excellent technical infrastructure.
- Critical data will always be stored in a secure place and backed up daily.
- All company staff will be attached to a high-speed electronic network that provides easy access to a variety of information and computing resources both within and outside the company.
- All information systems that contain or use critical information will be available on the electronic network.
- All hardware and software will be selected from a list of approved systems maintained by the Information Group.
- The Information Group will maintain a list of supported email, word processing, spreadsheet and analytical software.
- The Information Group will maintain a list of supported hardware and operating systems.
- The Information Group will define and publish information collection and maintenance standards.

Human component

- The Information Group will be chaired by the MD and will consist of Department Heads and the IT Manager.
- The Information Group will have overall responsibility for quality of information in the company.
- The Information Group will be responsible for ensuring that IT purchases comply with the IT architecture.
- The Information Group will be responsible for approving departmental IT budgets.
- Each manager in the company will be responsible for outlining a departmental information systems plan and budget with assistance form the Information Group.
- Every member of staff will have at least 24 hours of IT training per year.
- Clients may access the information stored in a secure area of our system.

Attention checker quiz!

1 What is the initial task of the Information Group when creating an Information Vision?

A To decide what technology to use ☐
B To talk to a wide range of people in the company ☐
C To immediately write the Information Vision ☐

2 Which of the following is not a category for the Information Vision?

A Technical ☐
B Human ☐
C Financial ☐

3 How far ahead should an Information Vision look?

A Two years ☐
B Three years ☐
C Five years ☐
D It depends on your company's business planning ☐

4 What does an Information Architecture provide?

A A hard and fast way of developing software ☐
B A telecommunications infrastructure ☐
C A framework of hardware, software and human elements around which future developments will be built ☐

5 Who should design the Information Architecture?

A The Information Group alone ☐
B The IT department ☐
C The Information Group but with greater involvement from IT ☐

6 If a department wants new software who do they approach?

A The IT Manager ☐
B The Information Management Group ☐
C The Finance Director ☐

In this chapter you will learn:

- what is a long-term information plan
- how to create a long-term plan from your business plan
- how to put in place a long-term plan

'Always plan ahead. It wasn't raining when Noah built the ark.'

Richard C. Cushing

What is a long-term information plan?

Three years feels about right to define as a long-term strategy. The rate of change in technology and in business is so rapid that a longer time span such as ten years would mean the use of a crystal ball. As we don't have a crystal ball, three years plus it is. It also ties in with your Information Vision and Architecture. The long-term information plan moves you another step towards the tangible rewards of successful information management.

A long-term plan can be defined as *'the way in which individuals and organizations set about achieving their goals'*. It involves using your resources to give you control of your environment. By extension then the long-term information plan is the way in which we achieve our information goals. A long-term information plan converts business objectives into actions.

So far so good. It's easy of course in the heat of battle to confuse strategy and tactics. In an ideal world the two are clearly defined and separate. In real life, however we have to respond to day-to-day pressures and events which may divert us from the grand plan. Don't get too hung up about this. The best way to cope is regularly to have a quick and dirty way of checking that the original goals are still in sight and short-term developments are within the framework created earlier.

Why do you need a long-term information plan?

Just as you want to plan for your business over a period of time so you are not pulled here and there constantly reacting to short-term issues, so too with information. It is expensive and wasteful to chase the latest fad and IT is certainly a fertile breeding ground for fads! (Having said that, in its early days some commentators likened the Internet to CB radio and dismissed it as a passing fashion). A good plan provides a sound framework for all IT decision making.

How to create a long-term information plan

Remember the reason for all this. Companies need accurate information, presented in a timely fashion, in an accessible format to make effective decisions.

The long-term information plan is a statement of major initiatives that the technical and business managers must accomplish over a defined time period to achieve the information vision. It must:

- be people focused
- be achievable
- be time bound
- identify measurable results to act as milestones for assessing progress
- complement the long-term business plan.

How to start

It can be a lonely process creating a long-term plan, so always look out for allies and people to bounce ideas off. Brainstorming is an effective tool for sparking ideas for your long-term plan.

One exercise that can be very effective is to use idea-triggering questions to identify strategic initiatives, as follows:

Who...

- Who can help or make contributions?
- Who must I sell on this idea?
- Who can help me get additional resources?
- Who will benefit?

What...

- What do I need by way of additional resources?
- What techniques or methods can I use?
- What is the best way?
- What is the first step?
- What will make the idea better?

Where...

- Where should I start?
- Where is resistance likely to be found?
- Where should I plant 'seeds'?

When...

- When should I introduce the plan?
- When should we implement the ideas?
- When should we revise the strategy?

Why...

- Why should people buy the idea?
- Why is this way better?
- Why is resistance so strong?

How...

- How can we improve on the idea?
- How can we test the waters?
- How can I persuade the existing centres of influence?

Four steps to creating a long-term information plan

We are now at that point where there is a blank sheet of paper in front of us and we've got to do something...

1 Conduct an external analysis

STEEP analysis

- **Social:** It is important to identify social and cultural changes which could affect your industry and organization. An example of this might be the growth of telecommuting, a facet of the 'Information Age', which will have an impact on your long-term information plan. This will also have effects elsewhere in the organization for instance in Human

Resources. Customers, being human, behave in strange and unpredictable ways – as shown by the rise of blogs as a communication tool.

- **Technological:** '*In five years' time all companies will be Internet companies or they won't be companies at all.*' (Andy Grove, Intel CEO.) Mr Grove made this prediction in the mid-1990s and his view seems to have been fairly accurate. It doesn't mean that you have to be a full blown 'only online' business but you do have to be aware of the opportunities and risks that are often amplified by technology. The Internet and Internet technology are giving individual organizations the opportunity to change their business model at relatively low cost. This can be a dangerous situation for companies who don't recognize that their competitors may not look as they expected and customers don't care where the service they are using comes from. An example of this is share-dealing online where virtual brokers are offering heavily discounted commissions on both US and UK stocks undercutting their traditional rivals.
- **Economic:** How will changing economic circumstances have an impact on your business and information plans? Is it worth bringing forward investment in information just in case interest rates rise further and more steeply than expected over the period of the plan?

  From a longer-term perspective we are undergoing a revolution in our basic economic structure. The core of the change is a shift from manufacturing to service industries, a shift from factories and capital intensive fixed assets to knowledge workers and tacit, intangible assets. Not only the service industry, by using the Internet for service delivery is affected by this. Manufacturing, through automating large parts of the production process, has also changed radically. Workers on production lines have been freed from monotony to contribute more of their knowledge and experience to improving quality.
- **Environmental:** As issues such as global warming and other symptoms of climate change become apparent technology may be able to help. If companies, where telecommuting was suitable, were given incentives to encourage staff to work from home a number of days a month, would you be ready

to take advantage of that? Preparing for such change is much easier if it is planned beforehand and budgets are in place.

- **Political:** Politicians like nothing better than to interfere in matters which they may or may not understand. Are there areas where political change (for instance in taxation) may have an impact on your business? In this case there is probably little that technology can help you with, bar hacking into the Inland Revenue's computer and changing your tax figures. However, this tends to be frowned on and isn't recommended.

Value chain analysis

This looks at where improvements can be made in the journey of a product or service from producer to consumer. It also includes your own suppliers and how that relationship can be managed to your advantage.

It is possible to gain competitive advantage by using technology to achieve the following:

- Inhibit the entry of new competitors by changing your product or service in the areas of price, perception, client service, product or service features. For example, by providing online service banks have (mostly) improved their clients' experience and reduced the cost of providing their service. However, the Internet has reduced cost of entry to the banking market encouraging new competitors to join the fray. This is a striking illustration of how competitive advantage can be short lived and companies need to continuously scan for the next opportunity.
- Build strong links with clients by removing obstacles for doing business with you. For example, the gambling industry has moved betting out of its old smoke-filled dingy settings and put it online. It is noticeable that it has become more closely associated with mainstream investing. Whether this is a good thing for our wallets is a different matter.
- Link closely with suppliers to reduce the cost of raw materials or services. For example, in the late 1990s Ford and Oracle created a supplier network Autoxchange™. The venture between Ford and Oracle linked Ford's 30,000 suppliers to the Internet and provided them with a means of participating in the manufacturer's development processes.

2 Establish long-term initiatives

Break the process down into three sections: clients, suppliers and competitors.

Clients

The key question here is how can we make life better for our clients?

- Are there ways to use IT to reduce our clients' cost of doing business with us?
  - By cutting back on paperwork and bureaucracy?
  - Providing information about orders more effectively?
  - By reducing the price of our service or product?
- Can we provide unique information to our clients?
  - Research about their industry sector
  - Research on their competitors
  - Research on future trends
  - Can we increase revenue by creating information products?
- Can we use external sources of information to find out more about our clients?
  - Through analysing questions the client has asked and identifying new services or products they might buy.
  - Through analysing the legislative environment.
- Can we use internal sources of information to find out more about our clients?
  - Do we know if any of our staff have worked for a client and can give us insight into the client's needs?
  - Is there a central point for this information?

Suppliers

- Can we use IT to reduce purchasing costs?
  - By searching for comparative quotes on the Internet?
  - By downloading software directly reducing postage and packing?

  - Buying directly from the manufacturer?
  - By finding substitute products?
- Can we use IT to reduce the cost for suppliers doing business with us?
  - By invoicing and receiving receipts online?
  - By giving them product feedback and helping them research their market in exchange for discounts on their products?

Competitors

- Can we use IT to raise the barriers to entry for new competitors?
  - By adding an IT element to our product or service. For example, electronic research newsletter.
  - By providing improved client service using IT. For example, servicing clients via a shared Internet site.
- Can we use IT to differentiate our services or products?
  - By drawing attention to existing differences?
  - By creating new differentiators?

3 Conduct an internal analysis

Use a **SWOT** analysis to do this. Identify the following:

- Strengths
- Weaknesses
- Opportunities
- Threats

Also, carry out a **technology assessment**. The impact of new technology on a company can be far-reaching, for example where innovation gives significantly improved quality or substantial cost reductions that cannot be achieved with existing techniques.

4 The Plan!

Identify a limited number of critical success factors. Be realistic – focus on what will work and will deliver immediate benefit to the bottom line. Take, at most, six critical success factors. Below is an example. Do this for each of the following categories:

- Clients
- Partners
- Suppliers

Clients

- Within three years we will service all clients over the Internet.
- Within three years new and existing clients will be supplied with information on their industry and other relevant developments via research reports which will be delivered to all devices including handheld ones. These will be chargeable at a rate to be decided.
- The most tedious or time-consuming administrative elements of the service process will be automated and done online by the target date.
- All billing, invoicing and payments will be performed electronically.

Partner companies

- We will execute 50 per cent of our transactions with partner companies by the target date.
- We will reduce their transaction costs and ours by 12 per cent through online collaboration by the target date.

Suppliers

- We will use the Internet to identify alternative products.
- We will use the Internet to get comparative quotes.
- We will reduce our costs with suppliers by 10 per cent.

Tips for a successful long-term information plan

Keep it simple

Don't aim for impossible targets. Improving corporate profitability is a more practical goal than building state-of-the-art IT solutions. Adding unnecessary complexities, such as adopting irrelevant technologies or focusing on trivial problems, can leave you stranded.

Mind the bottom line

Remember that the point of all this is to deliver better results, not to get the latest technology for its own sake (although the latest technology may sometimes be the route to improved profitability). Don't neglect a cost–benefit analysis. If the plan isn't going to deliver value don't do it!

Phase your efforts

Don't try to do it all at once. Break big projects up into small segments. Make sure the milestones and key success criteria have been achieved before releasing the next tranche of capital.

Focus on what works

Concentrate on solving priority problems first. Avoid doing things that go against your company's core philosophy. That will result in services your customers or staff won't really use.

Manage your suppliers

Dealing with multiple vendors is inevitable as you try to find the right technology to improve your business processes. But to minimize potential headaches, stick to a vendor you can trust and resort to others only when your chief supplier isn't able to supply something that's needed for a specific job. Have a 'gold standard' of suppliers with whom you have good relationships and can trust. Whatever the number, manage vendor relationships carefully to avoid muddling your strategy with conflicting products and visions. Don't let suppliers dictate your strategy.

Encourage an open culture

Making new developments work depends on the involvement and cooperation of employees at all levels and across all functions. Fostering communication across traditional departmental divides aids problem solving and helps ensure that integration benefits you and your customers.

Anticipate change

Easier said than done! The Internet, IT technology and business needs will all change rapidly over the next few years. Create a strategy that provides a clear framework yet that's flexible enough to accommodate the inevitable upheavals. If you are focused on information rather than technology this will be easier. Information needs are not going to be quite as much at the mercy of sudden, disruptive changes. Put together a small team to analyse new developments and match these to the business plan or identify where new technology might present an opportunity. For example, who would have foreseen that people could make money selling virtual real estate in 'Second Life' the virtual online world? Again the business benefits must be spelled out clearly and the means to achieving them must be clear.

Attention checker quiz!

1 Which of the following is not an attribute of the long-term information plan?

A People focused ☐
B Non-measurable ☐
C Time bound ☐

2 What is an effective tool for getting ideas for the Long-term Information Plan?

A Research ☐
B Meditation ☐
C Brainstorming ☐

3 In a STEEP analysis a change in taxation for IT contractors comes under which heading?

A Political ☐

B Economic ☐
C Technological ☐

4 Which of the following need to be part of a long-term initiative?

A Competitors ☐
B Government ☐
C Clients ☐

5 What is a practical maximum number of critical success factors?

A Twenty ☐
B Six ☐
C One ☐

6 What should you focus on for a successful long-term information plan?

A Information ☐
B Technology ☐
C Complexity ☐

09 the medium-term plan

In this chapter you will learn:

- **what is a medium-term information plan**
- **how to define objectives for the medium-term**
- **how to put in place a medium-term plan**

'Create a definite plan for carrying out your desire and begin at once, whether you are ready or not, to put this plan into action.'

Napoleon Hill

Now that you've put together a long-term plan for IT it's time to focus on more detail and move to the next phase, the medium-term plan. This is where you select the projects that will help you achieve the objectives of the long-term plan

What is a medium-term plan?

A medium-term plan covers a timescale of roughly 2 years. If you need a little more time than this don't worry – you know your own business and how quickly things can be done. You know the information architecture towards which you're working and a real plan is coming into focus. The medium-term plan differs from the long-term plan in that it:

- is more specific
- has clearly defined objectives
- focuses on how to achieve those objectives
- is a plan for actual systems such as:
  - email
  - standard desktop applications
  - operating systems
  - specific departmental software and hardware needs.

How to create a medium-term plan

1 Set objectives for the medium-term

First you have to identify in what areas you want to set medium-term objectives for your organization. Some examples of areas on which to focus are suggested below (and if you just follow these without going any further you're probably ahead of most companies):

- Improve staff satisfaction with IT services
- Supply all staff with a networked PC
- Improve robustness and security of information
- Reduce time taken to resolve support problems
- Upgrade email software to allow online sharing of diaries
- Create a secure online database of clients' details
- Improve availability of IT services
- Increase number of staff trained in essential software
- Increase speed of Internet access
- Improve ability to communicate electronically with clients, partners and suppliers
- Give staff secure remote access to company network.

The medium-term plan is where you decide which systems will achieve your long-term objectives. It is where you identify, specify and source hardware and software. Clearly it is an important part of the planning process. It is also where ill-defined specification can lead to problems later on.

2 Identify factors that will decide which projects get the green light

How you choose which projects to go for depends on a number of things:

Availability of resources

If the company has little or no capital available then its ambition has to be limited. Equally, if the number of IT staff on whom they can call is small, projects either have to be outsourced or deferred. Don't let lack of resources deter you – it just requires more careful project planning.

Potential of the project to fulfil the objectives

The project must have outcomes that clearly address an objective. For example, installing firewall software to protect the corporate network directly relates to the objective of improving robustness and security of information.

Risk

Playing it safe with low level incremental improvements may be very comforting but it isn't going to help a company gain competitive advantage. Using the objectives outlined above, this table breaks the objectives down into different categories of risk. When assessing risk in this case ask the following questions:

- Is the project going to be expensive?
- Will it take up a lot of people's time?
- Will it have an impact on other systems?
- What are the consequences if it all goes wrong?

Risk assessment for objectives

Objective	Risk factor
Improve staff satisfaction with IT services	Medium
Supply all staff with a networked PC	Medium
Improve robustness and security of information	Medium
Reduce time taken to resolve support problems	Low
Upgrade email software to allow online sharing of diaries	Medium
Create a secure online database of clients' details	High
Improve availability of IT services	Low
Increase number of staff trained in essential software	Medium
Increase speed of Internet access	Low
Improve ability to communicate electronically with clients, partners and suppliers	High
Give staff secure remote access to company network	High

and of course...

Politics

Depending on your point of view, politics is the art of getting things done or the art of stopping people doing things you don't want. By choosing staff from across the company for the IT Board politics at a department level may be less of an issue. Politics will often rear its ugly head when one group (whether justifiably or not) feels they are losing out to another. The best advice on this is to be open about the plans, consult widely and above all communicate with them clearly. Once the medium-term plan is ready, publicize it. This is where the members of the IT Board earn their extra coffee and biscuits! They will champion the changes needed and communicate the plan to colleagues. Run workshops where people can ask questions about the projects. This also (hopefully) instils a sense that the company is planning ahead for IT.

3 Prioritize projects

To help assess which projects need to be scheduled first it is a good idea to subdivide them under the following headings

Quick fixes

These will gain you immediate benefit. Target issues that are making people's lives miserable in the organization. For instance, is there someone who is struggling with a slow PC and therefore unable to complete their work on time and to the necessary standard?

Another example might be installing a new fast printer to replace a slow one. These projects build trust in IT.

Examples from the objectives:

- Supply all staff with a networked PC
- Increase speed of Internet access
- Give staff secure remote access to the company network

Slow burns

These projects deliver benefits of course, but over a relatively long time period. It is important to keep people informed as to progress on these. It is also key that they are managed in the same way as other, more concrete projects.

Examples from the objectives:

- Improve availability of IT services
- Increase number of staff trained in essential software

Day-to-day

These are the basic projects, necessary but not very exciting.

Examples from the objectives:

- Reduce time taken to resolve support problems
- Upgrade to email software to allow online sharing of diaries

Riskier (but possibly leading to competitive advantage)

These projects may be more complex and resource hungry but can help deliver competitive advantage.

Examples from the objectives:

- Improve ability to communicate electronically with clients, partners and suppliers
- Create a secure online database of clients' details

4 Manage the human side

The following are important points when managing the human aspect of developing your medium-term plan:

- Consult with all those people who will be using the systems every day.
- Communicate any problems immediately.
- Let the users have a strong voice in designing the software. This really is critical. If people feel they have had a major say in the design of a system they will be more willing to see it through the ups and downs of development. If they can see the benefits they will become enthusiasts for change and ensure it happens.
- Let them test it at all points. It's surprising what benefits can spring from this. Those staff with a detailed understanding of the functions that a system should perform will also be able to suggest other features to improve it.

5 Identify the following software needs:

- Who needs what and how will it be implemented?

- Off-the-shelf or bespoke – pros and cons of both?
- Will the new software run on existing hardware and if not what impact will this have on your hardware needs?

Summary

It is all very well having great plans for IT but most people are busy with the day-to-day stuff so you need to generate enthusiasm for IT in your company. During the medium-term planning phase, before the visibility of the short-term or implementation stage, is the perfect time for a programme of educating staff and preparing them for IT change.

These are some ideas from the real world for raising levels of interest in IT.

- Email a Friday afternoon IT question to all staff on a specific topic with a specific prize (a bottle of wine usually gets a response).
- Regular IT newsletter
- IT 'surgeries', where staff can drop in to ask questions or check out problems that may not be critical but they would like answered. It can also be used for brief training sessions on a specific question about a software application.
- Instigate a regular IT survey – again a prize for the first five people to respond. This will give you a clear idea of what and where the issues are.
- Move IT staff around different departments so they gain experience of all elements of the organization. Giving one IT person responsibility for a particular area boosts morale and gives them insight into the problems a department may face. For example, rather than disparaging Marketing for not being able to use a particular piece of software, IT staff will see the problem at first hand. They will be able to identify who needs what training in the department and even carry out ad hoc training sessions. It also provides an early warning system for potential issues on new systems before they become major problems. The only drawback to this approach is if the IT bod 'goes native' and becomes too involved, getting absorbed into the day-to-day work of the other department. It can be a fine line between helping someone with an IT problem and finding you are doing their work for them!

- At-desk training when required. Again this works well as a way of helping people over a specific issue. For instance, if someone hasn't done a mail merge in Microsoft Word before, they probably don't need a full blown course in the product but just need to be shown that function.
- Encourage IT staff to be fully involved in the company. Don't treat them as outsiders. Talk to them about advance planning, especially potentially disruptive ones such as office moves. I know of one company where a group director sprang a surprise on the IT department by deciding to move 20 members of staff into another building giving just a week's notice (it must be said he hadn't told the department that it was moving either). With more than a little blood, sweat, tears and toil this was accomplished but more prior notice would have made it a more successful and happier move.
- If you have a company bonus scheme include IT staff in it. It may not have occurred to you that they *shouldn't* be included, but one major company only rewards 'core' staff. I can think of no better way to destroy morale than this. If you've had a particularly good year or your company has grown big enough to have a bonus scheme, include all the service departments. Nothing is more divisive than the core being rewarded while those on the 'service' side receive nothing. Ask this question: could the core have performed as well or at all if they hadn't had support from IT, building maintenance or finance? Here endeth the sermon!
- Inform all staff in advance about any planned downtime of systems at weekends and make sure IT staff are flexible on this point. People are frequently under pressure of deadlines and have to work at least part of a weekend (bear in mind people working from home or remotely). Ask IT to set out a schedule of maintenance for main servers for each quarter. Perhaps one weekend per quarter will be enough. Email the schedule to all staff and repeat the email at the beginning of each month. The benefits of this are:
  - Servers have frequent maintenance
  - There will be less unscheduled downtime
  - Staff can plan their workload around this schedule
  - General staff feel their workload is respected and planned for.

Top tip

If you want people to buy into your idea, if possible, show them it! Telling people about a great new IT solution means little. Find a company that's actually installed it, made it work and is benefiting from it. Then wheel in the people you need to impress (those whose job function will be most affected) and let them ask questions of their counterparts. Better still, let them actually get their hands on the new system. If they love it you've got some very powerful allies and advocates on your side. They will also be able to articulate the benefits more clearly. On the other hand, if they hate it you've just saved time and money and avoided Project Management Hell for which you should be eternally grateful!

Attention checker quiz!

1 What is the usual timescale of the Medium-term Plan?

A Six months ☐
B Two years ☐
C Four years ☐

2 Which of the following is a factor for giving a project the green light?

A Enthusiasm for a particular technology ☐
B Potential of the project to fulfil the objectives ☐
C Requirement to spend extra money in the budget ☐

3 When assessing the risks involved in a project is upgrading email software seen as:

A High risk ☐
B Low risk ☐
C Medium risk ☐

4 Which one of these projects is a 'quick fix'?

A Increase number of staff trained in essential software ☐
B Create a secure online database of clients' details ☐
C Increase speed of Internet access ☐

5 Who should test new software?

A The people who will use it ☐
B The IT department ☐
C The software supplier ☐

6 Which of the following is a benefit of moving IT people round the company?

A Boosts IT staff morale ☐
B They can identify where training is required ☐
C Better relations between IT and business functions ☐
D All of the above ☐

the short-term plan

In this chapter you will learn :

- **what is a short-term information plan**
- **how to define objectives**
- **how to make the plan work**
- **how to manage a short-term plan**

'Work that counts gets implemented. It's that simple.'
Tom Peters

What is a short-term plan?

Now that you've been through the sweat of assessing where you are with information, have created an information vision and distilled it into a medium-term plan, you come to the bit where you have to roll up your sleeves and get your hands dirty. Or rather your IT team or systems provider do. At this point it is also worth appointing one person as a watchdog to document the project and also to keep an eye out for problems between team members. This has the following benefits:

- the project team can learn from the ups and downs of the project
- the watchdog provides a neutral voice who can assess issues objectively
- their documentation will provide a learning tool for future projects.

Before starting, take a moment to congratulate yourself and your colleagues on coming this far.

This then is the implementation phase of the plan that will deliver benefits to your organization. It needs sponsorship from the top, or through the IT Board who will control the individual parts of the plan. Remembering your project planning lesson, break the implementation down into phases.

How to define objectives for a short-term plan

From the medium-term plan the IT Board or project group will have identified whether the present IT infrastructure is adequate or whether upgrades are needed in key areas – this is a checklist:

Hardware

- Are the network cabling and hubs up to the task?
- Are the central servers up to the tasks that will be demanded of them?

- Is security adequate?
- Is better hardware needed on people's desks?
- Is faster Internet access needed?

Software

- Is the new software compatible with existing operating systems and applications?
- Are staff competent in the software they are using now?
- What software training is required? If so when and how will this be delivered?

Human

- Who will project manage?
- Are staff trained to use the software effectively?
- Will staff need training in the new software? If so this must be done as close to the installation date as possible so that new skills are not forgotten.
- Do IT staff have the necessary skills to implement hardware and software and manage the changes?
- Are extra (temporary?) staff needed for the upgrades?

Project management

Is a project manager required? One may not be essential if the project is a very modest one. It is still useful though to have, if not a project manager, a coordinator as a central point of contact. If your ambitions are on a larger scale you will need to appoint someone to oversee the project to make sure deadlines are met, objectives are fulfilled and budgets are carefully managed. Is there anyone on your IT team who has project management skills? If not can they be trained to take on the role or do you have access to anyone else who can fill this position?

Financial

- Will hardware be bought outright or leased?
  - If you are a small company, budgets are tight and you are only planning to buy a few PCs it is worth looking at Dell's outlet store. Here you can find computers that, for

example, have been returned due to faults and repaired or have been returned due to an incorrect order. They are brand new machines, in perfect condition but discounted.

  - If capital outlay is an issue you can also lease personal computers and servers from hardware makers. A leasing agreement can roll on so that every three years (for example) your PCs are replaced with the latest models. For more details on leasing contact the hardware manufacturers directly.

- Can existing software licenses be upgraded rather than new ones bought? Several years ago one canny company director took advantage of an offer by a major software company who offered a very cheap upgrade if you moved from an existing word processing package to theirs. He went onto the Internet, got 200 copies of a freeware word processor and used that to gain the upgrade!
- Are there licensing agreements available that will reduce the cost of buying software? Major software manufacturers such as Microsoft offer discounted prices through volume purchasing agreements – in Microsoft's case their offerings are called Open Licence or Select depending on how many licences you require. Usually there are discount points at various levels; for example, at time of writing, 250+ licenses trigger the Microsoft Select agreement. As licensing guidelines and regulations change on a regular basis it is worth checking the producer's website before you buy.

Questions to ask include:

- Are you getting the best possible deal on your software?
- Do you have to buy all the licences at once or can you estimate the licences you may need over a period and gain discounts on this basis?
- Is your company part of a larger group that may already have a software purchasing agreement in place?
- It's also worth talking to colleagues in the same industry and finding out where they buy software and what deals they get.

One cautionary note at this point. Don't buy a home edition version of software, for example Microsoft Works rather than Microsoft Office, just to save money. This may seem appealing because it is cheaper but it may limit what your staff can do and as you grow it can inhibit their performance. Home versions may also be less robust and have less support than 'industrial strength' software. The extra support burden on your IT staff may cause them to burn effigies of you!

Time for action! Implementation

... or how to make the short-term plan work.

Once all these issues have been resolved it is time to get things done. This is where you implement the systems that will achieve the objectives. Implementation is a word that can strike fear into the hearts of even the bravest. It really isn't that bad (honest).

Some companies blindly jump in and start implementing without thinking about the consequences. This section will guide you through how to make implementation painless (or nearly painless). You've been through all the effort of planning and preparation, and now it's time to see the rewards for those efforts.

Look at risks and how they can be reduced

Where major work is needed, such as cabling or installing a server, try to plan (if possible) for this to happen over a weekend as this will result in least disruption to staff. Again communication is vital. At the start of the week preceding major work, warn staff that next Monday morning may be disrupted, allowing them to get critical tasks out of the way in good time. On a more cheering note, modern software is more reliable and hardware more robust. If planning has been good and preparation adequate then there should be few if any problems with installation or upgrading.

Useful questions to ask are:

- If new hardware is needed, when will this be delivered?
- Can this be phased – if you have limitations on storage space, will storing it securely be a problem?
- Are there personnel issues? If for example you have 20 computers arriving and you have only one IT support guy, who is going to help him unload, check, unpack, store and

install the machines? Splitting it over a longer time period might be a more practical solution. In this case schedule who is going to receive which PC and when and communicate it clearly. Managing expectations is key to building trust and good relationships between IT and the business.

Note that laptops are an especially sensitive area. The term 'personal computer' means just that. A computer that is used by just one person. Multiply this feeling of ownership by a large number for laptops. As the owners of these are by definition going to be more mobile, they will probably have unique settings on their computers and will have them customized to work in their own way. If a new laptop arrives and is significantly different in how it works from a previous machine, this can be detrimental to productivity. There are two ways of addressing this problem:

Firstly, create a policy, in conjunction with your IT staff, setting out what will and will not be allowed on a laptop. Perhaps all laptops will be set up in exactly the same way and changes can only be made by authorized staff. This can be enforced by not allowing the laptop's owner to make any changes to the computer. A policy like this may prove rather rigid though, but varying levels of access to the laptop's setup can be allowed so that a member of staff who is comfortable with changing settings can be given permission to do so.

Secondly, buy a product such as Ghost where previous settings can be copied and transferred to the new machine, allowing your staff to benefit from the performance improvement and are immediately familiar with their new machine.

- Who will set it up? If there is new or bespoke software, is installation included in the price or is the installation process simple and clear? No matter how good your support team, they will be tackling a number of issues already with new hardware and software. If problems can be anticipated and planned for it will relieve the burden on their shoulders.

Tips

1 If possible it is worth setting up a 'lab' situation where IT staff can install the software beforehand to discover any problems. Remember that the conditions have to be as close as practically possible to the real world. Make sure it is the

same operating system and similar hardware to the ones they will be installing on later.

2 If possible get in the *actual* hardware and software early to give the IT team time to install, test and retest systems. It is then just a matter of swapping over to the new system.

A striking example of unanticipated consequences faced one company where software installation instructions were incorrect and the IT team wasted three days attempting to get a system working. Finally the supplier sheepishly admitted that there were 'a number of errors' in the manual.

- When will upgrades to the network be done?

If you are installing a few desktop computers this is not an issue as they can be done in the normal course of their work. Servers and major installations are a different matter. These really need to be installed out of work hours if possible. Using the lab to preinstall before systems go live will help but even with this cautious approach things can still go wrong. When planning the implementation phase it is worth having a 'paranoia' meeting where you go through scenarios of things that can go wrong. This also keeps people thinking and alert as to potential problems. One office manager was renowned for her faultless office moves and at the heart of it were a series of such meetings.

- Are there any unforeseen security issues as a result of installing new servers?

Although this will have been covered in your medium-term planning it is important to consider whether anything has changed since that time. A new server may have additional logins and passwords which need to be disabled. Don't feel you're alone in this. In the mid-1980s one American organization set up a new server, made sure everyone involved had a secure login and password and changed the password every week. Their only oversight was that the server came with a 'backdoor' login of 'guest' and the password was... 'password'. These had not been disabled leaving the server wide open for three months. This might have been embarrassing for, say, a retailer or computer company. But the organization was a nuclear missile base. They are still not admitting who got access and it is unclear what information was revealed.

Finally, remember these crucial points:

- It is critical to manage people's expectations and make sure they know when their new hardware and software will be delivered so they can prepare for it.
- Are suppliers ready to deliver on the dates you have specified? When assessing this, take into account lead times for different services such as broadband which may require a few weeks' notification of installation. One of your staff should be given the task of coordinating suppliers. For example, a broadband and telephony supplier may need to talk to your telecommunications provider about installation dates.
- It is critical that your IT people are briefed and there are no surprises in store. One organization planned on moving a team from one building to another only a hundred yards away but had not told the IT manager. There was no network link between the two buildings and the team was about to be stranded without easy access to critical information. The head of IT called in favours from suppliers allowing him to order and install a wireless network between the two buildings over a weekend but it was a close call.

Bite-size chunk time!

Once again breaking it down into manageable chunks will help not only from a planning but also a budgetary point of view. Costs can be spread across the period of implementation. Hardware can be leased which moves costs from the capital budget to running costs.

Phase 1: Months 1 to 3

There are three ways of installing new systems:

1 The Big Bang

This involves setting a specific date for when the entire company will move to a new system. The old system will effectively be switched off and everybody will use the new system.

Pros:

- Clarity – everyone knows they should be using the new system and when it is going to happen.
- There is no duplication of effort – one day information is input into one system then it is transferred across and the next day it is input into the new system

Cons:

- If the new system fails it is difficult returning to the old system as information may be lost.
- Staff acceptance of the new system has to be absolute.
- Training has to be comprehensive.

2 Parallel running

Parallel running means you run the new system alongside the old one and check that you are receiving the same output from both (of course they *could* both be wrong but it's unlikely they will be wrong in exactly the same way).

Pros:

- Clearly this is a safer way of launching a new system especially where it is critical to the business or could have catastrophic consequences.
- People can gain familiarity with the new system while still using the old one.

Cons:

- This is very inefficient and labour intensive. Information has to be input into both old and new systems and checked at every stage of its process.
- Human nature being what it is, people will cling to the old system as a comfort blanket and adoption of the new system may be delayed. This has to be managed carefully with specific milestones for acceptance of the system and a definite switch off date for the old system.

3 Pilot scheme

A pilot scheme involves installing a new system with a small group of staff and monitoring closely their experience. A core of these staff will have been involved in choosing and testing the software. Once they are happy with how the system is working and it is fulfilling all the criteria decided on at the outset, the system can be rolled out to a greater number of staff. Finally it is installed across the company.

Pros:

- Easily controlled and if there are problems these are limited to a small number of people who have been consulted in advance and are key members of the implementation team.
- If the pilot group has been involved from the outset they will be able to troubleshoot any problems and describe issues in detail to the IT team (this is a major advantage in fixing problems).

Cons:

- The system may work well with a small number but fall over when rolled out further so success in the pilot group is not an absolute guarantee that all is well (although it is a good indicator).
- There might be incompatibility issues between existing software and that used by the pilot group.

Planning

The following planning method aims to make hardware and software installation as safe and easy as possible. It is the plan–do–check–act method, illustrated for phase 1 of our example scenario:

Plan:

- Identify and recruit pilot group(s). It is advisable that a pilot group is an extension of the original team who initially researched and tried out systems thus creating the pilot groups around a core of product champions. Brief them extensively.
- The network cabling will be replaced and a new server installed.
- Send tender to three suppliers and get quotes for network cabling.
- Send tender to three suppliers and get quotes for new servers.

Do:

- Install network cabling.
- Install new server.

Check:

- Review performance of network.
- Review and monitor server performance.

Act:

- Resolve any problems.
- If all is working to the parameters set in the medium-term plan go to phase 2.

Phase 2: Months 4 to 6

Plan:

- Schedule installation of hardware and software and training.
- Train staff on new software.

Note that training must be done *at the same time as installation* so that there is no time lag between people being trained and them using the software.

Do:

If you are using a pilot group:

- Install new hardware and software in pilot group.

If you are not using a pilot group, set up a test lab and install hardware and software.

Check:

Review progress. Identify problems.

Act:

- Resolve issues.
- Once everything is working to the satisfaction of the organization, roll out to a larger group.
- Go to phase 3.

Phase 3: Months 7 to 9

Plan:

- Schedule further training sessions where necessary.
- Schedule remaining installation work.

Do:

If you are using a pilot group:

- Consult the pilot group and find out what is working and what is not.

If you are using a test lab:

- Review the test lab and install hardware and software.

Check:

- Monitor progress on the installation of hardware and software. Inevitably this is when problems begin to rear their heads.
- Develop a checklist of problems and allocate responsibility for solving them to specific people or teams.
- Review progress regularly.
- Make sure the IT team has the resources available. If they seem to be struggling with a particular difficulty, are they capable of fixing it themselves or is outside help required?

Act:

- Resolve any issues with the pilot group or in the test lab.
- Once everything is working to the satisfaction of the organization, roll out to a larger group.
- Go to phase 4.

Phase 4: Months 10 to 12

Software

You need to consider the following issues:

- What further training is needed? How will training take place, who will perform it, in-house or external?

- Are grants available? It is worth contacting your local Chamber of Commerce or Business Link about grants and other resources for retraining staff?
- Bear in mind training for IT staff as well!
- Maintenance and support contracts for software – upgrade policies.
- Budgeting.
- Risks – system transitions.
- Controlling projects.

Hardware

In these final months, you need to consider the following hardware issues:

- Specification.
- Standards – establish and enforce policy.
- Lease or buy? Pros and cons of both.
- Support implications.
- Staffing levels for IT support.
- Training needs – training needs analysis – internal or external training.
- Not just PCs – network hardware such as routers, hubs and switches.
- Security implications.
- Backups.

One month before implementation

This is a critical time to keep communication channels open. Send emails to all involved giving dates when installation will take place. Warn staff that there may be disruption but with their cooperation and the level of planning that has gone into the project this should be minimal. It is also worth holding a question and answer session so that staff can have their concerns directly addressed.

Two weeks before

Send another email repeating when the installation will take place and giving more details such as phone numbers for support.

One week before

Another email (preferably from a senior manager) should be sent reinforcing the previous ones. This time it could have a checklist attached that will clarify exactly what people must have done by this time.

After the project

As it is unlikely that this is the last project the organization will ever undertake (unless it's been a complete disaster) it's worth looking back and identifying how well it worked so the team can learn from the experience. At this point the watchdog presents an overview of the project and how well it has achieved its objectives.

Attention checker quiz!

1 The short-term plan could also be called?

- A Initiation phase ☐
- B Information phase ☐
- C Implementation phase ☐

2 What is the most cost-effective way of buying software?

- A Through a volume license agreement ☐
- B On a machine-by-machine basis ☐
- C Letting each department buy their own ☐

3 When is the best time to install a major network component?

- A Monday morning ☐
- B Wednesday evening ☐
- C A weekend ☐

4 What could you do to give the IT team a chance to iron out bugs before installation?

- A Train them on critical software and hardware ☐

B Let them set up a test 'lab.' ☐
C Both of the above ☐

5 Which of the following is an advantage of installing a new system with a pilot group?

A Clarity – everyone knows they should be using the new system and when it is going to happen. ☐
B Easily controlled and if there are problems these are limited to a small number of people who have been consulted in advance and are key members of the implementation team. ☐
C People can gain familiarity with the new system while still using the old one. ☐

6 When installing a new network server what may have changed and must be taken into account?

A Power supply ☐
B Security ☐
C Warranties ☐

how to recruit a high-performing IT team

In this chapter you will learn about:

- the attributes of a high-performing IT team
- preparation for interviewing staff
- effective interview questions
- how to motivate an IT team

'Few great men would have got past personnel.'

Paul Goodman

Many managers see IT people as a breed apart and indeed quite a few IT people seem determined to maintain the image. In reality, IT people are very like all your other staff. They will respond well to incentives but what motivates them may be slightly different from other people.

The attributes of a high-performing IT team

The attributes of a high-performing IT team include these:

- Able to identify and solve technical problems.
- Pre-empt major hardware and software problems through good planning.
- Work well together and share knowledge.
- Good at explaining to staff what they have done to fix a problem thus reducing the chance of it happening again.
- Able to train staff where relevant.
- Have a broad range of skills.
- Enthusiastic for their work.
- Creative thinkers.

It's a tall order to find people with all these attributes but they are out there. It's up to you to find them. If you just want to pay the lowest salaries possible then it's easy to find people, but you will have an equally low performing team. Pay some more and you will have a team capable of driving IT forward and improving productivity.

Recruiting a high-performance IT team

There are two main tasks involved in choosing someone to fill an open position in your organization. First, you must assess a candidate's technical skills, and second you must judge how well the person will fit into your organization and work with others.

Types of staff you are likely to recruit

Basic support staff

When hiring at an entry level, you will be able to offer a lower salary, but there may be significant tradeoffs. An entry-level candidate should come to you with a solid educational background and possibly certification, but will likely have little or no on-the-job experience doing the work you require. These new workers will have difficulty solving problems because they don't have problem identification and solving skills. In addition to technology issues, entry-level candidates may also lack business skills, leading you to ask yourself whether the candidate will be able to handle customer problems and complaints and instil customer confidence in your business.

Experienced technical staff

Your second option is to hire an experienced candidate, who will have higher salary expectations. The adage 'you get what you pay for' often applies here. An experienced hire will be productive almost straight away as they will have problem identification and problem solving skills. Nor will business issues be foreign to them. If you hire the right person you should be able to delegate a task and pretty much forget about it. It also needs to be someone you get on well with as none of us gets any enjoyment or is fully productive working with people we don't like.

To find experienced talent, you have a number of options. One of the best methods for finding a reliable person is to start with your personal network. The upside of this is that it is free. The downside is that you might risk losing a friend if you don't like the candidate or have to let them go later on. Other options for finding experienced talent include hiring an agency or recruiter, newspaper, Internet job postings, and CV searches.

IT Manager/Director

A good IT Manager needs to have technical skills plus the ability to interpret business needs into technical plans. They must be self-motivated and able to plan and execute projects on time and within budgets. He or she will also be a key member of your Information Group and therefore must have good interpersonal

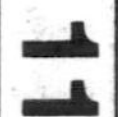

and political skills. The IT support team will be under their direct control so an ability to motivate diverse characters is important as well. They must be able to communicate with people at all levels of the organization. There is probably a good chance they will meet your clients. A personable, credible individual is essential for this role. Get the right person in the job and IT management becomes much easier.

Interviewing: technical vs interpersonal skills

The level of technical expertise a job candidate needs depends on the job the person will fill at your company. An entry-level help desk technician, for example, may need more customer service skills than solid technical experience, while a network administrator may require more proven technical skills.

How good are the candidate's technical skills?

Understandably this is always a tricky area for general managers. If possible, you need someone who has at least an awareness of the relevant technology sitting with you. The interview questions you ask to determine technical proficiency will vary depending on the position you need to fill. For a helpdesk technician, you may want to check his or her experience in specific areas, such as the Internet or email. If you're interviewing a candidate for the position of network administrator, you will ask questions specifically related to technical knowledge and problem resolution skills, such as, 'A member of staff complains that when she prints a document in any application, the printer output is garbage. What is the most likely cause of the problem?' Bear in mind that technical skills can be taught, but if someone is poor with people then you may have more of a problem.

How good is the candidate with people?

Finding people who are technically good is important but you need a team with members who will get on with everyone in the company including Keith in Accounts and Sheila in Sales. Think of the most difficult individual in your company and imagine how the interviewee might get on with him or her.

You need to know how this person will adapt to the environment and how well the candidate will work with others to accomplish changing goals in the organization. There are libraries of books out there that advise people on how to answer the most typical interview questions and therefore many candidates are well rehearsed. So how do you break through the candidate's façade and find out what you really want to know? You ask open ended questions that are designed to find out more about the candidate's work ethic and fit within the organization. For example:

- Tell me about your role in a team you have worked with in the past.
- How did your role affect the success of the team or project?
- Tell me about your most enjoyable time working with another team member or with a member of staff?
- How have you handled negative feedback from clients, customers, or team members?

Useful interview questions

These are by no means exhaustive but are a start point:

1 **How hard and on what projects have you been working lately?**

2 **How do you react to being told 'No'?** This is going to happen to IT people a lot in their careers, especially when there are constraints on budgets. A positive response would be if they said they would take it with good grace and suggest alternative projects that deliver value for less cost.

3 **Are you able to say 'No'?** This is essential to manage the workload in a support role. It's too easy to say yes to every demand, even unreasonable ones and end up with a huge 'to do' list and no time to do it!

4 **Honestly, how good are you at coping with change?** Everyone has some sort of answer ready for this one. Ask them to give a clear example of managing change from their experience.

5 **Are you a good improviser?** Being able to improvise and think on your feet is a crucial skill for support staff.

6 **What have the last couple of years taught you?**

7 **How do you stay up to date with changes in technology?**

8 **What's the toughest thing you've had to do professionally?** This question also comes out of the interviewing playbook, but it's still a good one. I'm curious to see if the candidate

mentions some technical achievement or project or discusses something more personal instead (for example, having to fire an employee).

Interviews are tough for everyone – for the job seeker and for the manager seeking the perfect candidate. The process can be particularly stressful if the person you are looking to hire is a high-level appointment. In that instance, there is much more involved in conducting an interview and evaluating job candidates and an agency may well be worth the fee!

Prepare, prepare, prepare

Before you meet any candidate, get prepared well before the interview – perhaps even by calling candidates in for low-key discussions. Make sure you, or someone who can sit in with you, know the skills, both technical and personal, that are needed to perform well and that you're clear on the objectives and your expectations for the position. Prepare written interview questions. Many executives choose to have HR or an outside executive recruitment firm do an initial screening.

Setting the tone

Put the candidate at their ease so that they feel they can answer more openly. Conducting interviews away from the office, perhaps in a local coffee shop might be an option. One company almost recruited a candidate who was technically brilliant but temperamentally utterly unsuited, a fact which only came to light when the IT Director invited him out for a drink with the Finance Director. The lesson is, don't assume any candidate will just fit into your company culture and don't be blinded to a candidate's faults by their technical ability.

Some tips on conducting effective interviews

- Categorize the skills you want for the role into three areas:
  - technical ability
  - interpersonal skills
  - motivational skills.
- Read up on the applicant's education, experience and knowledge before he or she comes in for interview.

- Spend more time on interpersonal skills than technical ability.
- Have a plan for the interview but be prepared to deviate if something interesting comes up.
- Take notes during the interview to help your recollection afterwards.
- Allow plenty of time for questions.

After the interview

For senior roles such as IT Manager or Director, it's worth getting other colleagues who will be working with the person to talk to the applicant as well so that there is a balanced and broad-based appraisal and consensus on their suitability for the job.

How to motivate IT staff

Motivating an IT person is much the same as motivating any member of staff. Find out what their interests are and where possible base the allocation of tasks around those interests.

Amongst other things, consider the following:

1 **Create variety:** This applies especially to IT support staff. Support can be monotonous and in fact if IT staff are successful in reducing problems on your network it becomes more so. Of course they have to continue to support the company's IT but there may well be time for more interesting projects as well. The most valuable thing a leader can do to motivate is to assign work to people who have an interest in specific areas. For instance, if you discover that one of your IT staff is an expert in databases find out where in the company there might be a need for a database and assign him or her to the project.

2 **Give the big picture:** Make sure the IT team understand the significance of their work to the company as a whole and how what they do helps.

3 **Show a career path:** Work with people to give them goals for their careers. Be specific about what competencies they must demonstrate in order to advance their career.

4 **Encourage teamwork and transfer of information:**

Transferring knowledge between the people in a team has multiple benefits, including:

- It motivates people as they feel supported and part of a group working towards shared objectives.
- It protects the company against the loss of an individual and the knowledge they possess.
- If the information transferred is stored and made accessible to others it will build over time into a valuable asset for solving technical problems and training new staff.

Attention checker quiz!

1 Which is **not** an attribute of a good IT person?

A Pre-empts major hardware and software problems through good planning ☐
B Expert in arcane cabling systems ☐
C Good at explaining to staff what they have done to fix a problem thus reducing the chance of it re-occuring ☐

2 Entry level IT staff may lack what?

A Problem solving skills ☐
B Business skills ☐
C Hands on experience ☐
D All of the above ☐

3 Which of these is not a recommended method of finding experienced technical staff?

A Train the guy who works in the post room ☐
B Use an agency ☐
C Use your personal network ☐

4 Which should you spend most time on in an interview for IT people?

A Technical ability ☐
B Interpersonal skills ☐
C Motivational skills ☐

5 You notice the support team are getting bored: what might be a good way to motivate them?

A Give them more money ☐
B Send them on an away day ☐
C Give them a project in an area that interests them (and is beneficial to the company). ☐

6 You wish to appoint an IT Director. Who should interview him or her?

A The HR Director ☐
B The CEO ☐
C A range of senior staff who will work with the recruit ☐

12 disaster recovery and security

In this chapter you will learn:

- **what is disaster recovery**
- **how to create a security management system**
- **how to put in place a disaster recovery plan**

'When anyone asks me how I can best describe my experience in nearly forty years at sea, I merely say, uneventful. I never saw a wreck and never have been wrecked nor was I ever in any predicament that threatened to end in disaster of any sort.'

E.J. Smith, Captain, *RMS Titanic* (writing in 1907, five years before his brush with the iceberg)

Disasters come in all shapes and sizes. This is no less true for computers than anything else. Major disasters such as terrorist attacks, earthquakes and hurricanes are the ones that attract attention. Yet they are few and far between. Unfortunately this rarity leads to complacency as demonstrated by the unlucky Captain Smith. For most of us damage to our main computer systems comes from a spilled coffee or careless road menders cutting through a power cable. These are the smaller, more frequent problems that damage client relations, hurt productivity and lose revenue. They also result in frustration, mistrust of computers and may jeopardize the acceptance of future projects.

Of course we need to protect ourselves in case the worst does happen therefore this chapter covers:

- Disaster recovery and business continuity
- Security of information

Disaster recovery

Disaster recovery (DR) describes the ability of the business to get back on its feet and running normally as quickly as possible after a major disruption of service due to events outside the company's control. We'll base planning and preparation on a worst case scenario. Disaster recovery planning and its costs are like insurance, we don't see a return on our money but it is a necessary service that we hope we will not have to use.

Prevention

To protect our companies against disaster we need to reduce the chances of anything happening to us in the first place. Work out what is and what is not within our control. There are a few preventive measures that we can put in place. This means that at least we have reduced the risk of problems.

Anti-virus software (for servers, desktops and Internet email)

Anti-virus software monitors computers for any software which may pose a threat to that machine or the network. Trying to remove a virus that has infected your network is time consuming and damages productivity. It's better to stop viruses before they strike by subscribing to a service that checks your Internet mail before it arrives in your inbox.

Recommended service: MessageLabs

Identify, buy and install solid backup software

Backup software creates a copy of your information, usually on to a tape and in the event of a major problem such as a server crash, you can fix the hardware then restore your information. If that sounds too easy you're absolutely right! Backups are only as good as the people who do them and the software that runs them. I know of one company where a backup had not been done for four months leaving them vulnerable to massive data loss. With ever increasing amounts of information on our networks, they also take longer to backup. Therefore companies often backup data incrementally, in other words only the information that has changed is backed up.

Regularly check the effectiveness of your backups by restoring test data onto a server

Of course a backup is also only as good as your ability to restore from it. This is why it is essential to regularly test backup procedures by restoring randomly chosen computer files and making sure those files can be accessed and read.

Keep backups offsite in a secure place

There is no point having perfect backups if they are then kept in a place where they are vulnerable to damage or theft. Taking backups home is all very well but there are issues of security where ex-employees may still have data tapes (albeit out of date ones) at their homes. The tapes may also not be kept in an ideal environment in terms of heat and dust. Data may also be at risk from theft at home. There are companies which provide secure collection and storage of backup tapes.

Recommended service: Recall

Make sure critical servers are in a locked, safe environment

Often the most obvious weaknesses are missed when we talk about protecting systems. Although they have become much more robust over the years computers are still sensitive to extremes of heat and cold. It is advisable to keep servers that are critical for your business in a locked room where the temperature is controlled. It's also advisable having them in racks with access to the back – this makes life easier for your IT staff when there are problems.

Install protected power supplies on all critical hardware

Power failures and spikes are frequent especially in city centres where construction work and road repairs have been known to cause power supply problems which can cause severe damage to computers. Uninterruptible power supplies (UPS) are must-have items to smooth the flow of power to a server and provide battery backup in case mains power fails. The server can then be closed down properly, avoiding damage and data loss. It may also pay to identify other computers and hardware (for example a graphic designer's PC) where a UPS is necessary. You can buy them for standard desktop computers or (more powerful and more costly) for servers.

Recommended product: American Power Conversions

Develop a disaster recovery plan

A disaster recovery plan will scale from minor incidents, such as loss of one server for a short period to complete loss of access to the building. An outline of DR planning follows this section. Advance preparation makes it much easier to deal with a crisis when senior staff will be extremely busy and under stress.

Identify a disaster recovery service

This will allow the company to move key staff to another site where work can continue. Identify what percentage of the company needs to be relocated.

Protect against the most likely problems

If there is a server (possibly email) that must be kept running at all times it is worth looking at companies that provide instant reinstatement of service. If a server crashes with a hardware problem (failed hard disk or processor) the first couple of hours is often taken by the internal IT team trying to fix the problem. Once it becomes apparent the problem is hardware related then it could be another day before a part can be shipped to you. Instant reinstatement means you can be up and running within 15 minutes of the original problem.

Recommended service: Capital Continuity

Provide secure remote access

In the event of a major incident, key staff with access to the company network can work from their homes or other offices and support the effort to recover from the problem. This can be of benefit if there is a major incident and you do not have access to your premises.

Disaster recovery planning

Scope

Firstly assess what you can and cannot control. If something (a major terrorist incident for instance) is outside of your control, focus on recreating your office in a new location rather than worrying about the old one which is out of action.

Analyse the risk

You can prepare for the most likely risks by asking these questions:

- Where do the main risks come from?
- Are you in a high crime area?
- Are you in an area that is likely to flood?
- Do you have frequent power outages?
- Are you in a potential terrorist target area?
- Are there ex-staff (or indeed present staff) who bear a grudge towards the company?

The following grid helps to analyse priorities:

Low probability–low consequence	**High probability–low consequence** ■ Power failure
Low probability–high consequence ■ Major terrorist incident ■ Earthquake ■ Flood *Example:* 11 September 2001	**High probability–high consequence** ■ Hardware failure ■ Software failure ■ Theft ■ Fire (with attendant water damage) ■ Deliberate act of sabotage ■ Human error *Example:* ■ The email server goes down when you need to send a critical document to a client ■ Failure of finance system at month or year end

Planning

- Create a 'bunker team' – this comprises key individuals such as CEO, Office Manager, IT Director, Finance Director and HR Director and relevant department managers.
- Decide in advance what the minimum staffing levels are for each department. Again remember that this may differ depending on business cycles. Prioritize issues, for example:
  - invoicing – critical for maintaining cash flow
  - payroll.
- Give a number of individuals the task of calling specific company members informing them of the situation. They in turn call a given number of colleagues so all staff are kept fully informed of events.
- Assess where else risks may exist. For example, if a key supplier had a major failure how would this affect your

business? Or if one of your main clients was put out of action and could not pay invoices how would that affect your cash flow. One example of this was the earthquake that severely damaged the Japanese city of Kobe in 1995. A major centre of semiconductor manufacture, it left computer makers short of chips and sent semiconductor (and PC) prices rocketing. The effect was especially acute in those companies practising just-in-time manufacturing who had low inventories of memory.

If you have not got the resources to subscribe to a disaster recovery service with a backup site there may be less costly ways of doing this, for example:

- Are you part of a larger group of companies who could share offices in the event of a disaster?
- You could have a mutual arrangement with a supplier or even a client.

Real life example 1

I have seen this final point work to great advantage for an organization. One major service company had a client in London Docklands who suffered catastrophic damage in the Canary Wharf bomb. Fortunately there were few and very minor injuries but having recovered from the initial trauma they had no office to use. Their supplier called to say that they had set up a temporary office in their offices using old personal computers but with all the necessary software, email access and had arranged for phones to be put in. In effect they had created a mini disaster recovery site and the client was up and running from their temporary home next day with their core team. They were able to maintain cash flow, talk to their customers and generally keep the business going during a difficult period. The client 'camped' at the supplier company's office for a fortnight while a new permanent office was found. Around six months later the supplier came up for review and it goes without saying that the client was more than happy to renew their contract.

Real life example 2

It's always the big spectacular events that make the headlines but one devastating event left an office unable to work for days. Sixty staff arrived for work one morning to find that their personal computers would not start up. The odd machine failure here and there is not unknown but for such a large number to fail at once is unusual. Initially the IT department got the blame until it was discovered that a gang had broken in during the night, removed memory chips from all the computers and had very carefully replaced the covers. At the time memory was extremely expensive and the thieves got away with some £12,000 worth of chips. But the cost to the company was probably much more than this headline figure, with lost time, lost business and the intangible of damaged customer goodwill.

DR planning is a continuous process

Planning for disaster recovery is an ongoing task, so consider the following:

- At least once a year (and preferably every six months) go through your disaster recovery plan not only with the IT team but also managers from across the company and make sure it is up to date. Most properly thought out plans make specific arrangements for older systems, smaller applications, and other systems that tend to fall off the importance radar over time.
- You need to find out from each department or the entire business in the case of smaller organizations, exactly what software and hardware they're using, as well as that which they no longer use. Determine the priority that your executives place on each of the remaining systems. This quick, informal review will allow you to move on to the next part of the process.
- Once you've established your priorities, eliminate unnecessary items from your disaster recovery plan. This will lessen some of the burden on your technical people who may currently be giving life support to redundant software and hardware.
- If possible, reassign licences and services to new systems that

require Disaster Recovery. In addition, utilize the freed-up hardware to ensure that these new systems have the redundancy they need. Since the hardware and licences are already paid for, the finance guys will think you're a miracle worker for saving tons of cash while still meeting the requirements of the organization's information systems!

- Spring cleaning for DR and HA systems also has the benefit of creating financial savings that go directly to the bottom line. It also allows you to properly protect new systems that have been introduced since your last review. This is a strong argument to be used during tough budget negotiations and it might even earn you a gold star from your Finance Director!

Security of information

Data theft is an increasing problem for companies. We've all received or at least read about 'phishing' emails where individuals try to get you to divulge the details of your bank account or a Nigerian prince has an inexplicable desire to park $40,000,000 in your bank for a few weeks. These are the headline grabbers but most theft of information is more mundane and for that reason, a far greater danger to your business. In fact your data is at greatest risk from internal forces. To identify and put in place measures to reduce the risk of your company falling prey to the theft of information take the following steps.

Evaluate risk

It's possible to become so paranoid about security that you almost stop the use of information in your company thus defeating the purpose of having all that valuable information in the first place. It's a useful exercise, therefore, to ask:

- Does your organization operate in a sensitive sector?
- Are you working with information such as customer or staff records which come under the Data Protection Act?

What do I need to do under the Data Protection Act?

If you are required to comply with the Act, you have a number of legal responsibilities:

1 To notify the Information Commissioner that you are processing information, unless you are an organization who has personal information only for:
   - staff administration (including payroll);
   - advertising, marketing and public relations for your own business; or
   - accounts and records (some not-for-profit organizations).

(*Source:* The Information Commissioner's website.)

2 To process the personal information in accordance with the eight principles of the Act; and

3 To answer subject access requests received from individuals.

If you have any doubts about your responsibilities under the Act call the Information Commissioner or check their website.

Laptop and notebook computers

A Chief Executive once said, 'Of course the problem with laptops is that they are so easily carried.' A slightly surreal and surprising comment perhaps but he hit on a core fact. What makes them convenient for legitimate owners applies equally to thieves. In the context of security, laptops are a minefield. With ever bigger hard disks they can contain a vast amount of information that is the lifeblood of your company and could be invaluable to an unscrupulous competitor. The FBI estimates that a lost laptop '*represents a loss of $86,000 in information value*'!

You can protect them by following a few simple guidelines:

- Only provide laptops for people who really need them, not as a perk.
- Mark laptops with an invisible or ultra violet marker so they can be returned to you if stolen. This also helps the police to identify stolen computers and prosecute the criminals.
- Make sure information on the laptops is backed up regularly.
- Install a product such as Deadman's Handle to disable access to information on the laptop.
- Ensure that access to the corporate network is password protected on laptops (it should be on all machines but especially so on these).

Remote access

As home and remote working become more prevalent it is necessary to open your network up to those staff who need access to centrally held information. Clearly this is a security risk but a relatively simple one to eradicate. Therefore, you need to:

- Make sure remote login is secure and use of a unique login and password is enforced.
- Install a firewall that hides your remote access from the Internet.

Employees

Employees who leave the company (whether voluntarily or not) should have access to the computer network stopped on their last day (this is usually done by a system administrator changing the password). If they have personal information they wish to take with them, the IT Manager or system administrator must deal with it. Some companies go further with a policy that from the day an employee resigns they have only restricted access to information on the network. For example, they do not have access to shared information. This is a thorny area and really if you cannot trust an employee when they are leaving, why did you employ them in the first place?

Key security policy elements

Logical security

- Computers should have the most up-to-date software security installed, in line with the level of acceptable risk. For example, installations that allow unrestricted access to resources must be configured with extra care to minimize security risks.
- Adequate authentication and authorization must be provided, proportionate to the use and the acceptable level of risk.
- Attention must be given not only to large systems but also to laptops and handheld computers which, if stolen or mislaid, could pose a threat to the organization's information. This should include computers belonging to a small group or for an individual's personal use.

Physical security

Appropriate controls must be employed to protect physical access to resources, proportionate to the level of acceptable risk. These may range in scope and complexity from extensive security installations to protect a room where server machines are located, to simple measures taken to protect a member of staff's screen from being overseen. Physical security is easily overlooked as was demonstrated by one Finance Director (mentioned earlier) who, although very hot on IT security, left an original document showing directors' salaries in a photocopier.

After all the scare stories and threats out there remember that your IT systems are there to help your company. Put in place the level of security that matches the level of risk that your company may face. There has to be a balance between the level of security and making it easy for you and your staff to access systems. Bear this in mind when planning security and you won't go too far wrong.

Attention checker quiz!

1 To allow your company to retrieve data what should you install?

- A Anti-virus software ☐
- B Backup software ☐
- C A firewall ☐

2 Where should backups then be kept?

- A The IT Department ☐
- B The Finance Director's safe ☐
- C Offsite in a secure location ☐

3 What should be installed on all critical hardware?

- A Batteries ☐
- B Uninterruptible power supplies ☐
- C Alarms ☐

4 In the context of disaster recovery which is a high probability/high consequence event?

- A Major terrorist incident ☐
- B Flood ☐
- C Theft ☐

5 What do you need to provide to let key staff work from home?

A Secure remote access ☐
B Another site with similar hardware and software to your original office ☐
C A permanent duplicated office on your own site ☐

6 What is the name of a product which disables information on a stolen laptop?

A Checkpoint One ☐
B Personal Firewall ☐
C Deadman's Handle ☐

13 the money

In this chapter you will learn:

- **how to put together a budget for IT**
- **where to make savings, and where not**
- **about total cost of ownership**
- **about hardware and software deals**
- **about making money from IT**

'Because that's where the money is.'

Willie Sutton, US bank robber on being asked why he robbed banks

'I spent a lot of money on booze, birds and fast cars. The rest I just squandered.'

George Best, giving his take on fiscal prudence

Budgeting for IT

Budgeting is one of the places where the gap between general management and IT management is most noticeable and causes most, er, 'discussion' for want of a better word. The conversation often goes something like this:

> Finance Director: 'So what sort of budget are you thinking of for next year?'
>
> IT Director: 'Well we need to implement a new intranet and install wireless networking in Marketing. That's in addition to CRM across the organization, laptops and Blackberries for all staff and three new servers. I guess half a million should do it.'
>
> Finance Director. 'That sounds fine. I'll just sign a cheque and let you fill in the figures.'

Now if you're alert you may just have discerned a slightly unreal or even sarcastic tone in that fine bit of dialogue. In fact what the Finance Director will be thinking is something along the lines of the following:

'What on earth is all this stuff, why does it cost so much and what will it do for our bottom line?' Oddly enough that's *exactly* the question everyone should have been asking from the outset.

Budgeting should be an integral part of the information planning process from the very start, giving your company the chance to:

- Assess different ways of paying for IT.
- Prepare, request, scrutinize and negotiate tenders without being under time pressure.
- Uncover any systems that are unrealistic, too risky or will not deliver benefit to the organization.

How to put together a budget for IT

1 Budgeting and controlling IT costs

It's very easy to get into budgeting as a ritual. Usually around September time the Finance Director has a chat with the IT Director and they come to a chummy agreement that this year's budget will be the same as last year's plus maybe 2 per cent. There are a number of flaws in doing things this way.

- The IT Director will spend all this money whether he needs to or not, knowing that to underspend will reduce the budget figure for the next year.
- It assumes that the company's activities this year are exactly the same as last year.
- The IT Director may well be too optimistic and not request enough money.
- The IT Manager or Director may engage in 'budget padding' to add a bit of slack into the budget figures thereby guaranteeing money will be wasted.
- It means that when radical change is needed and more investment required in IT this will be a fraught process.

2 Setting a budget

Good Planning = Good Budgeting

Start setting the budget early and involve the Finance Director in the planning team so that she or he can see IT strategy developing and get a feel for what investment might be needed. If they are fully involved they will also be able to use their experience to suggest ways of funding projects that might not occur to other team members.

A budget is a dynamic item and is an estimate of anticipated costs. Once you have developed your three-year plan then you can start putting together a reasonable overview of budget needs for that period.

The following guidelines will help you in setting a budget that achieves your aims:

- Be realistic in your goals.
- Fit your budget to *your* needs and plans, not someone else's no matter how persuasive they may be.
- Identify where you may be able to cut costs and which elements are essential.
- Remember to include the unexpected; an example of this might be costs related to a new client who requires tighter security.

What investment will move the company forward?

The Information Architecture will identify specific hardware and software requirements for which budgets are required. Once you have identified these you can schedule spending. Don't be tempted or pressurized by sales people into buying before you need to (unless they offer a very deep discount) as generally hardware prices will drop over time. You may be able to negotiate a keen price with them if they are aware that you will be buying a certain level of software or hardware over a given timescale. The corollary to this is, don't put off projects just because you think that prices will be lower next year. If staff are being held back and productivity is falling due to old PCs you need new ones now! If a project will move your use of information forward significantly then do it without delay.

Quick fixes and critical issues

Target areas where you most need immediate investment to gain quick payback. For instance identify problem areas where there are productivity losses or vulnerabilities that could adversely affect the company's performance. The following could well be top of your list of suspects:

- **Storage issues:** Are your network servers running at full capacity in terms of storage space and how can this be fixed?
- **Email storage:** Often the email system gets used as a filing system (we've all done it by storing emails with attachments rather than saving the attachments to our personal directory on the network). An upgrade to the email server may be needed. This might be a housekeeping issue where people need guidance and training as to the correct place to keep

attachments and where to store old emails. Bear in mind that we need to keep important emails not just for our own records but as a legal requirement.

- **Security issues:** Is the network at risk from intruders? If so this is not a place to scrimp on investment. There are however cost-effective tools out there that will protect your information.
- **Downtime:** Are you losing productivity due to the network frequently not being available? Do you lose access to email on a regular basis? If this is the case you need to allocate money to resolve these problems.

Total cost of ownership

For IT to gain credibility it has to deliver value to the organization. IT is often seen as a cost centre. One reason for this is TCO. Just what you wanted, another acronym! **Total Cost of Ownership** is the bane of the budgeter's life. One of the major shocks to any company is realizing how much a PC really costs to run. This is where the *Titanic* of your budget meets the iceberg of unseen cost! It is true that the price of hardware has dropped significantly over the years and manufacturers are now offering servers for £299 – but what they don't say is that for the server to work effectively you have to add another £800 or so but that's still a lot less than the £10,000 that you would have paid a decade ago for a similar machine. It's on the desktop though that total cost of ownership really kicks in. The current average annual total cost of ownership of a PC is around £5,000! Much of this is hidden in maintenance and staff costs. A PC may cost only £250 to put on a desk but the ancillary costs of software, support and upgrading will add at least another £500 to the price. Another issue is that we tend just to count the capital costs. Once you start counting salary costs of IT staff, maintenance agreements, training, downtime and depreciation and the iceberg begins to reveal itself in all its glory. If you really want to assess the TCO, estimate the following costs:

- Hardware
- Software
- Annual depreciation on hardware and software

- Computer supplies – printer cartridges, CDs, cables etc.
- Any hardware and software lease costs
- Salaries of IT staff
- Maintenance contracts on servers and desktops
- Training on software
- Consulting fees
- Outsourcing
- Software development
- Internet access
- Email services
- Lost productivity due to computer downtime (this by its nature will have to be an estimate).

Then take a deep breath and divide the total of this little lot by the number of PCs in your organization.

Purchasing policy

Part of the problem is one of perception. If you don't understand IT then it can seem like a black hole into which money gravitates never to be seen again. Give the multi-disciplinary Information Group the task of putting together a simple policy for purchasing hardware and software, encouraging people to follow these guidelines:

- There must be three comparative quotes for hardware and software.
- Use product and price search software on the Internet to find the best deals.
- The Information Group must be involved in all hardware and software purchases over a certain value.

3 Managing a budget

Breaking projects down into milestones and only releasing funding on the completion of each one helps control costs. Inevitably though there will be areas where budget requirements change. Whether these revisions are up or down (how often does that happen?) they should be:

- documented by the planning team with dates and reasons for the change
- the effects of the change (especially if it's an upward revision) may make other projects unfeasible

Review the budget regularly. Look for areas where you can make savings. Here are some ideas.

Online and direct purchasing

Buying online directly from the manufacturer avoids the mark-ups of the middleman. Dell Computers was an early proponent of selling directly via their Internet site and slashed PC costs by doing so. They realized earlier than their competitors that PCs had become a commodity. As PCs have become connected to networks of all shapes and sizes they have grown into communication tools as well as processing devices. Oddly and happily for all of us they have become cheaper as well.

Check your maintenance agreements

It's worth asking the following question. Why do we need maintenance agreements for PCs?

A company in London had around 200 PCs and every year they were paying around £70 per machine for maintenance, thus giving a computer support company a tidy £14,000 for doing, well very little in fact. On investigation it was found that there had been one hardware problem with a PC over the year – a screen had failed and had been replaced with a spare, costing roughly £80. As noted before, PCs have become a commodity and as one IT Manager remarked 'would you have a maintenance agreement for all the staplers in your company?' Why not buy, say, two spare PCs at a cost of around £300 each and replace any hardware failures with them in the increasingly unlikely event of failure.

Where you do need maintenance agreement is on servers which are critical to your business.

Budgeting on a shoestring – where to reduce costs

Standards to reduce support costs

Establish a standard for PCs so that parts likely to go wrong can be kept in store thus removing the need for expensive maintenance contracts. Computer hardware today is in general very reliable. Just to reiterate, you do need maintenance on file servers and other hardware that keeps your business alive.

Regular audit of IT

This will identify the following:

- **Redundant systems:** It is not uncommon to find an old system that hasn't been used for a long time but no one has thought to turn off. There may also be old systems that only one or two people use and are a disproportionate drain on time and money. Assess whether the job can be done by other software and if so get rid of the old system.
- **Software licences – too many or too few?** It is important to stay legal and have one licence for each use of the software. There may however be software for which you only need a few licences across the company as no more than a few people use it at any one time. For example, this might apply to research software. If staff numbers have declined in the last few years are you still paying for licences that are no longer needed?
- **Is there duplication of software?** This can happen where there is no policy on software purchasing and departments buy their own. Has another department got the same software? If so check to see if their agreement allows cheaper upgrade for extra licences.

Auditing also prepares you for upgrading hardware and software. If you know exactly what assets you have and their age it makes budget planning easier as you will have a fair idea of when they need to be replaced.

Software deals

What are you spending on telecoms? How can these costs be reduced?

Voice over IP

If you have staff working from remote sites, home or a branch office and want to reduce the costs of communications with them it is advisable to think about connecting them using telephony over the Internet which can be low or even no cost. This could also be a solution for your communications with clients, suppliers and partners.

The main providers are:

- Skype www.skype.com
- Vonage

Can you make contra deals with clients?

If for example you have an IT or a telecoms company as a client can you take part of your payment in goods or services from them?

Example from the real world

One software developer working with a client, a garment manufacturer in Saudi Arabia, was able to reduce their client's cost of doing business by:

- Hosting a stock control system on their own (the software developer's) server. Previously their client had used an in-house bespoke system which was complex, expensive and difficult to support. Most stock control functions, apart from printing bar code tickets, were now performed at the developer's site and the clients could get on with manufacturing.
- Using voice over the Internet for IT support significantly reduced international phone bills.
- The software house was also able to help support and train client staff by remotely accessing their desktop computers.

What can go wrong?

Where do you want to start? Budgeting is one area where the fault lines between business and IT are most obvious. If the Finance Director doesn't understand IT or isn't involved in the planning process she or he may see the function as a money sink where hard won revenue disappears for little apparent gain. One reason for this is that it is hard to quantify how IT impacts positively on the bottom line. Yet it does. It is in this area that both business and IT people really have to put in the effort to assess how IT can make money for the company. Part of the problem is that within departments people may notice better productivity or enhanced service but they don't have time to sit down and document in detail how IT has transformed the business process or added to revenue. Therefore much of the evidence is anecdotal and I'm afraid, IT Managers and Directors out there, it's your job to collect these testimonials and try to quantify the benefits in monetary value. The positive side of this is that your talks with the Finance Director will become a lot friendlier.

There are two main areas on which you can spend money on IT, as follows:

Keeping the show on the road

The nuts and bolts stuff that just keeps your company in business. Identify which parts of this can be commoditized, desktop computers perhaps. Money can be saved in this area while other elements of standard IT, such as servers, require more investment.

Making a difference

The best way to look at this is to give an example. The research department of a professional service firm swallowed a lot of cash through its sophisticated use of information systems and bespoke software. The Finance Director often felt he wasn't sure if he was getting value from the department but thought of it as a necessary evil. The head of the research department saw things differently and decided to see how the department could become a profit centre. For some time she and her colleagues had been producing a monthly research report for a client. She approached a friendly contact at the client and (presumably after a decent lunch) asked how much the client would be prepared to pay on the open market for the material they produced. Looking rather sheepish, the client replied that he'd wondered when she'd been going to suggest they paid for it as the information was invaluable to them! A sum not unadjacent to £200 per month was mentioned and the client happily paid up. The research head then approached other clients in a similar vein and began generating a healthy additional revenue stream for the company which more than offset her department's spend on IT.

Attention checker quiz!

1 Which of the following is a flaw in taking last year's budget and adding an arbitrary percentage?

- A It guarantees under-investment in IT ☐
- B It assumes that the company's activities this year are exactly the same as last year ☐
- C The IT Director may request too much money ☐

2 Where do the hardware and software requirements come from?

- A The Information Vision ☐
- B The Long-term Information Plan ☐
- C The Information Architecture ☐

3 What does TCO stand for?

- A Telecoms and Computer Operations ☐
- B Total Cost of Ownership ☐
- C Total Computer Operations ☐

4 On what hardware is it important to have maintenance agreements?

- A Desktop computers ☐
- B Printers ☐
- C Servers ☐

5 A purchasing policy might have which of the following elements?

- A There must be three comparative quotes for hardware and software ☐

B Use product and price search software on the Internet to find the best deals ☐

C The Information Group must be involved in all hardware and software purchases over a certain value ☐

D All of the above ☐

6 If you have a number of staff who work from home and a small branch office what might be a good way to save money?

A Use couriers ☐

B Use voice over the Internet for telephony ☐

C Give each of them their own server ☐

In this chapter you will learn:

- how to continuously improve IT
- what is knowledge management
- how to discover where knowledge is in your company
- how to convert knowledge into tangible benefit to the bottom line

'As for the future, your task is not to foresee but to enable it.'

Max Jakobson, Finnish diplomat

'The future cannot be predicted, but futures can be invented.'
Dennis Gabor, *Inventing the Future*, 1964

So far we have looked at how to:

- put a robust IT infrastructure in place
- create an information strategy that puts future decisions about IT on a firm footing
- devise a medium-term plan that sets out clear objectives for IT in your organization
- implement your objectives with a short-term plan.

So, where to next?

Continuous improvement

Having gone to all the trouble of planning and implementing a clear roadmap for information in your company it would be a shame to stop there. You have the mechanisms in place to keep ahead of competitors by monitoring developments in your company, your industry and in technology. How do you keep this momentum going to bring permanent benefit to your company?

First, keep the Information Group together to:

- Monitor technological advances and where these might affect your company
- Assess competitors and their use of technology
- Measure improvements in use of information
- Keep the momentum going behind using IT for business benefit.

Second, keep staff up to date and sell IT successes with:

- A regular newsletter
- Regular IT 'surgeries' where people can drop in for demonstrations of software or hardware.

Knowledge management

'We are drowning in information and starving for knowledge.'

Rutherford D. Roger

'A man who carries a cat by the tail learns something he can learn in no other way.'

Mark Twain

Remember the earlier mantra; it's all about information **not** technology? Well this is where you start to see why this is the case and reap the benefits. Once you've got control of IT you may well think you can put your feet up and relax. Not quite! It's now time to start using all your hard work to gain real advantage and squeeze the maximum from all that information in the heads of your people. Welcome to the world of knowledge management (KM). Or to give it it's real title, information management. Data is the raw material of information. Once it has been refined and sifted through the experience of skilled people it becomes information, then knowledge and finally wisdom. We are indeed drowning in information. The term 'knowledge management', is bandied about a lot these days. It can seem like another management fad which will disappear. Before you dismiss it as a passing fashion and if you want to know whether KM applies to your situation, ask yourself the following questions:

1 Do you employ people for their brain or their brawn?

2 Are you aware of where all the information is in your organization and what it's worth?

3 Are you selling hard-won information and knowledge to clients and if not, why not?

4 Would you like to turn the ideas in your organization into money?

If we're to understand KM and its potential for our companies, we need to ask some hard questions. We need to clearly define what knowledge could do for our clients (and us). One way of doing this is to identify problem areas where managing information can help. What problem(s) can we solve by better capture, distribution and using the knowledge that we already possess? Let's consider some examples.

Problem 1: Wasting time and money looking for information

Twenty-five per cent of your salary bill is wasted due to staff searching for information that *may not exist*. Another 25 per cent of their time is burnt up creating information that someone *has already done* (e.g. presentations). We *can* eliminate this waste, simply and cost effectively. Creating a central home for information that is as easy to use as a web page and organizes information by client, industry or whatever category best suits your business will significantly cut the time taken to find a presentation or other document.

Problem 2: Losing ownership of valuable intellectual property

By this time next year, 11 per cent of your company's value will *belong to a competitor*. *How?* If you are engaged in service activities around 90 per cent of your company's value is held in the heads of your staff. Let's hope they don't go to a competitor. The average turnover of staff in the IT industry in 2005 was around 12 per cent. They *have* gone to a competitor! It could be worse – other industries have a staff turnover closer to 20 per cent. If this doesn't worry us all, it should.

Problem 3: Throwing away valuable information that could be reused

Companies spend a huge amount of time and effort accumulating information during new business pitches and projects then often treat it like a waste product. This is valuable information that can be recycled and help with your next project or pitch. It is also a valuable resource for training new staff. Capture, organize, distribute and capitalize on it.

Real life example of success in these areas

A multi-national engineering company created an online 'University' where staff, partner companies and clients could access previous projects and case studies derived from completed projects.

Problem 4: Reacting to changing business environments

Competitors can appear from anywhere (the online stock broking industry is an example of this) and companies often have to change business practices rapidly. If you are concerned about being wrong-footed in this area you're in good company. Microsoft came late to the Internet party but realized its potential and rapidly realigned their business model to make all their products ready for the Web.

> **Real life example of success in this area**
>
> A company in the business of providing hardware and software for authorizing credit cards found that its practices had become bogged down in paper shuffling resulting in frustrating delays for clients and a less than happy workforce. Nimble competitors arrived on the scene and started eating into their client base, threatening the business.
>
> A new CEO made the company a virtual organization, eliminated paper and created an agile organization ready for the twenty-first century. On his own admission this was at times a painful process especially for staff who joined and had to get used to a company with no headquarters, no written documentation and business conducted by email. All corporate information is available online, worldwide, for immediate access. The company's top 250 people, for example, track sales down to the last week, the last day, even the last hour. Another database tracks which people speak what languages – a useful tool when doing business around the world. Another system posts the travel itineraries of everyone in the company, including flight details, hotel reservations, and phone numbers. The radical changes paid off with revenues rising 50 per cent year on year.

How to discover where knowledge is in your company

In the real world knowledge management is not about technology! It *is* about relationships, partnership and communications, made *possible* by technology. This is not the age of the Internet – it is the age of the client (the Internet just helps – a lot).

Just in case anyone still thinks knowledge doesn't matter, look at it this way.

How often have you heard the mantra, *'Your people are your greatest assets'*? In the last few years this has become accepted wisdom but, it could be argued, not accepted practice.

If people are not working with their hands (and in an increasingly service orientated economy this is becoming rarer) we prize them for their knowledge and expertise. Even when people do work with their hands it is their knowledge of the job that creates value. So why do we so often treat that knowledge like a waste product? One good reason is that information is intangible. If a managing director found the office manager was buying company cars then parking them in the car park never to be used again, it's quite likely he might politely ask what was going on.

Modern organizations are at least 75 per cent knowledge in the same way that the human body is 60 per cent water. Just as your health will suffer if you don't drink fresh water, your organization will suffer if you don't look after intangible but precious knowledge assets – the know-how of your staff. Ninety per cent of your organization's value walks out of the door every evening. And what about competitors trying to poach them and all that knowledge? Just think of the average cost of recruiting a new person, training them and getting them up to speed? And that is only the tip of the ignorance iceberg – you now have a huge gap in the company's experience.

With the web allowing us to work free from constraints of time and place, for relatively low cost, there's no excuse not to use knowledge effectively.

If this is all going to work you cannot do it half-heartedly. This isn't the time for incremental change. What is required is complete, fast transformation of your business. But you can do it safely through rapid prototyping. For this you need to:

- Recruit a pilot group
- Assess its use of information
- Start changing

- Ask 'Is it working?' If it is, rollout to the rest of the company. If not, find out what's wrong and fix it.
- Carry on to the next step.

Increasingly we are working together across the world and tapping into the knowledge of our peers. In this new business environment, rich communications tools are:

- Websites
- Intranets
- Extranets.

Swapping information in this way demands high performance, resilient networks to allow the exchange of multi-media material. Not only is the information becoming richer but also those with an interest in that information will widen to include clients, suppliers and the public.

Where does information live?

Most organizations see people as odd, messy things, to be dealt with through the Human Resource department and kept in the organizational equivalent of a chicken coop. Through this policy, flexible, skilled, intelligent staff get stuck in one unchallenging role. The wisdom to see this as a massive waste of valuable talent is a rare and exotic commodity. Yet how often, when we need fresh ideas, do we gallop off to the far horizon, pay big consultancies big money to tell us what we already know and then leave their report sitting on a shelf? This is management by ritual ensuring that nothing will really change.

But hold on a moment... There's a lot of brain-power right under our noses. Remember those staff you've barely seen since the Christmas party last year? They know the company, warts and all. They know their jobs. Most importantly, they know what would make those jobs better. That woman in accounts and the guy in IT are smart enough and think differently enough to create great ideas for other departments. It's just a matter of tapping into their talent, stirring people's curiosity and getting them to think about the company as a whole and not just their bit. Let's give them a really challenging brief. Transform the organization for the better!

Real life story

Now you're probably thinking, 'That is all very well but in the real world we don't have time.' Make the time! It will pay you back exponentially. One company assembled a group of volunteers form around the organization, gave them a blank sheet of paper and set them the task of looking at the company's future without preconceptions, limits, or prejudice. Who could resist that challenge? This resulted in:

- some whacky ideas
- some great ideas for the future
- a number of challenging initiatives which were truly different to the received wisdom in the organization.

It avoided the problem of 'not invented here', because people were willing to listen and try ideas when they could talk to the originator and give their own views on what would and wouldn't work. Yes, it needed good management to get it to work and keep the momentum up, but isn't good management our job? The payback for the company was:

- Motivated staff
- Smart ideas
- Transfer of best practice
- Agility
- Competitive advantage.

Attention checker quiz!

1 What is a function of the Information Group in this phase of a company's IT development?

A The members get involved in IT support ☐
B It assesses competitors and their use of technology ☐
C It is disbanded having fulfilled its function ☐

2 How can you keep staff informed about IT successes?

A At an annual forum ☐
B Wait until they ask ☐
C With a regular newsletter ☐

3 Roughly what percentage of your employees' time is spent looking for information?

A 25 ☐
B 50 ☐
C 75 ☐

4 In a knowledge-based business are we employing people for?

A Brains ☐
B Charm ☐
C Strength ☐

5 Which is not a rich communication tool?

A Corporate website ☐
B Paper based memo ☐
C Extranet ☐

6 What is a safe way of developing tools for managing knowledge?

A Rapid prototyping ☐
B Parallel running ☐
C Big bang ☐

project management

In this chapter you will learn:

- **how to identify which projects to do**
- **how to plan and control an IT project**
- **the attributes of successful and unsuccessful projects**
- **project planning tools**

'Tell me and I'll forget, show me and I may remember, involve me and I'll understand.'

Chinese proverb

According to Microsoft's Encarta dictionary a project is defined as *'a task or scheme that requires a large amount of time, effort, and planning to complete.'* You can say that again! At some point in your information planning you will find that you have a list of projects to get the organization moving in the right direction. Now you have to sift through them and decide whether and in what order, you are going to do them. In this chapter the sample project will be a customer database. On the face of it this is a relatively straightforward project. It will allow frequent mailshots to clients and automate regular communications such as Christmas card lists, notifications of new products and invitations to events.

Identify which projects to do

It is a role of the Information Group to identify possible projects from conversations with staff across the company. They will have produced a list of possible projects. Rarely will you have the luxury of doing a full analysis of each project. If a project is small and the Information Group is happy that it will bring benefit to the company they should have the power to give the go ahead.

For larger projects which require greater investment the group should present a brief synopsis of the merits of each project to senior managers. Where possible go and see an example of a similar project and talk to the people involved.

Prioritize

Some projects may be urgent, some can wait and some are not viable at all. Occasionally you will have a list of projects all of which have merit. A key area where minor IT projects fail is when too many projects are attempted at once. Saying 'No' is a skill managers have to learn. Prioritizing projects, communicating when they will happen and why helps manage expectations.

It helps to split projects down into categories such as:

- **Keeping the show on the road:** These will be clear from the start. If the group has discovered that the company network is not capable of reliably supporting staff or that an email server is constantly crashing then those are your urgent priorities.
- **Keeping up with competitors:** This of course assumes you know what your competitors are doing. Can you find out if you don't already know? Will the proposed project fulfil this brief? The customer database probably falls into the 'staying up with competitors' class and we will assume it gets the go ahead. It can be developed for a reasonable cost and will bring benefit to the organization.
- **Gaining competitive advantage:** Will the project get your nose ahead of your competitors? For how long? What happens when they catch up? Have you got more projects ready to drive the company forward?
- **Gaining industry leadership:** Are there projects that will put you so far ahead of your competitors that what you do becomes the standard for your industry? Be aware that even companies that have leadership will be caught sooner or later! It never stops does it?

With the IT board examine the potential project list and ask the questions:

- Do we understand what the project will do for the company?
- Do we have the financial, human and technical resources to do this project?
- Will the project bring major benefit to the organization?

Plan your IT project

Appoint a project manager

When appointing a project manager, bear the following points in mind:

- If the project is highly technical the project manager should come from a technical background.

- If the project will change the way the business operates it should be led by a business manager.

Create a project team

This team requires people with a wide range of skills. Getting a successful outcome with projects has been likened to herding cats, implying that you will be dealing with a number of individuals who wish to go in different directions, at different speeds and who may damage the furniture if they don't get what they want. Your team members will need to be:

- Good networkers
- Politically astute
- Persuasive
- Able to anticipate problems
- Motivated
- Smart.

Enthuse the project team

People, as always, are key to successful projects. If they don't want to do it, can't see the point or feel it will not deliver what they want then it won't succeed. Get the project team behind you by involving them from the earliest possible point. Make them feel it's their project, listen to their ideas good and bad. Take them out for a beer or a meal to get the team talking to each other. If the entertainment budget can run to a karting evening or an awayday so much the better.

Delegate carefully

One senior manager in a software company was notorious for sidling up to people and uttering the dread words, 'I've got a nice little project for you.' This could herald anything from overseeing the building of a new headquarters to looking after his dog for a weekend. He tended to dump the worst jobs on people and then criticize them when it went wrong. This isn't a great way to get things done. (By the way if you are unlucky enough to come across this character, choose the building project, the dog's a menace.)

Identify clearly the tasks and responsibilities that can be delegated. Take a look at your available staff before committing to delegation. If they are already working overtime to keep up with their workload don't overload them by adding more responsibilities. This is a certain way of ensuring project failure. Discuss the reasons for delegating responsibilities with the person who is to receive them and develop an implementation plan. It may be useful to share this discussion with the entire work team to receive feedback on how the process will affect everyone on the team.

Decide how the project team will communicate and how often

Email has transformed how we work and this will probably be the main communication tool. That's fine but if there are problems it is vitally important that people get together face to face to talk about the issues. That way there is less room for misunderstanding or passing the buck to someone else. Regular reviews are necessary to keep the project on track. Frequency depends on the size of the project and risk of the project.

Decide the scope of the project

Which parts of your organization will the project affect? Is it purely internal or are there external aspects to it? In the case of the client database there are clearly external issues as well. These may be legal as well as practical.

Define the project clearly

Legendary American investor Warren Buffett will not invest in any company where he cannot understand what they do. This isn't a bad way of looking at projects as well. If you don't actually know what the project does how can you explain it to others or gauge if it is successful or not? Break down what the project will do in detail so that everyone involved, the project team, those who will be using the system and you as a manager are clear on what exactly the project will and won't do.

Example

For instance the database project could be defined as:

1 We will create a database which will hold the following information: Company name, address, industry sector, contact details, personal information on our contacts there, whether they are an existing, former or potential client and other information necessary for our relationship with the company.

2 This information will be used internally by:
   - The new business team to find new clients and to analyse our client base by industry, geography and size.
   - By management for maintaining and improving relationships with existing clients

3 To make the database easy to maintain and for compatibility with existing software it will be developed in Microsoft Access.

4 We will either buy the software 'off the shelf' or have it developed by an external provider chosen by tender or have it developed by in-house IT resource.

Note: If you are thinking of having software developed for you, stop for a moment and ask yourself if it isn't possible to buy a package off the shelf that will provide most if not all of the functions that a bespoke development will give you. Bespoke may end up more expensive and it brings a greater element of risk to the project. If you are sure that the outcome you want is unique and no one else will have done it then look at bespoke development.

Create the project specification and get sign off on it

This is where projects can fall apart before they begin and we don't even realize it. There isn't a short cut here. Roll up your sleeves and start talking to staff who are going to use the system. In fact they have to be in on every stage of the system's design. It has to work the way they want it to **not** the way the developer thinks it should.

This point is also where the notorious *project creep* begins. If there is inadequate control over what is within the project specification, further down the line – usually just as you think the project is complete – something else will be required. In the case of the client database someone might ask for a module that will show the client's credit rating. Had this been agreed at the beginning it might have been easy but perhaps at this point it requires the additional cost and effort of designing and writing the extra module. You also find that this causes a bug which has an impact on another part of the system.

To avoid this scenario ask all parties concerned to sign off on the final definition of the project. There has to be a firm date set after which no fundamental changes can be introduced. Another critical part of the project specification is knowing when the project will be over and the system will go into its maintenance phase. A firm date must be set when the project's sponsors or champions will sign it off and hand it over.

Other issues will come out of this specification exercise, for example:

- Who will enter information?
- Who will keep this information up-to-date and accurate?

Note: With the example database development it must be made clear that entering information about clients is not and should not be the job of the IT department. This is the province of client-facing staff. Supporting the technical side of the database *is* the job of the IT department. These issues need to be addressed early on so responsibilities are clear cut.

Decide what will make the project a success

You must decide from the outset what will convince *you* that the project is a success. What outcomes do you expect and how will they show themselves? These need to be:

- Set by you and your colleagues *not* a supplier. In other words be clear in your own mind what *you* want to see come out of the project.
- Clear. Easily identifiable and measurable so there can be no ambiguity about whether something is successful or not. If you're not satisfied with it, completely, then that is not success.
- Communicated without ambiguity to those who are designing, developing, testing and implementing.

A project is a success if...

- It achieves its purpose
- It meets the specification
- It provides satisfactory benefit to its owner(s)
- It satisfies the needs of everyone involved
- It meets pre-stated objectives
- It meets budgets
- It meets pre-determined timescales
- It satisfies the needs of the project team.

Seven steps to a successful project

- Ensure there is a clear champion for the project
- Make the objectives crystal clear in advance
- There needs to be good governance of the project driven from board level
- The project team needs to draw people from across the company
- Brief the project team clearly, setting objectives, budget and timetable
- Manage expectations of all involved in the project. Are all expectations the same? Do they conflict? If so where and how can this be overcome?
- Make sure the relevant people are aware of all the systems the project must work alongside.

Controlling a project

Review regularly

Weekly reviews between the Project Manager and the Information Group are critical. If a member of the Information Group can sit in on IT team meetings even better as she or he may pick up on something that has been missed or may sense that the project is not going to achieve a key objective.

Use the work breakdown structure

Break the project down and deliver it in chunks allowing people to see progress is being made rather than deliver the whole thing all at once after a long period. Make sure success is communicated and celebrated. Reward those who have gone the extra mile.

Communicate progress

Let staff know how the project is progressing. If they are going to be using the end product they should be involved and kept up to date (with bad news as well as good).

What to do if a project starts to go wrong

From the beginning of the project let your project team and the leader know that honesty about problems will be appreciated not punished. If there is a blame culture in a company then that company should forget about projects. They just won't work. Worse, they may think everything is going fine but the truth is everyone is too worried to tell the truth. Open discussions about failure are essential so the project team can be alerted and act early on to solve problems.

How do you know a project is going wrong?

Keep an eagle eye out for the initial signs of problems. A minor task slipping slightly may not be a problem. But if that slippage means that another team member has to delay testing a module which impacts on an implementation milestone then there is a problem. A deadline looks as though it is going to be missed or during testing something doesn't work in quite the way it should. Requests for more money stretching the project budget suggest that unforeseen events are having an impact on the project.

Act quickly

Human beings are often overly optimistic. It is too easy to wait and see if a project is going to turn itself around. This immediately risks starting a slide towards discovering too late that something is wrong and missing deadlines in a vain attempt to correct it. Know when to intervene – there is a fine line between getting involved too early thus hurting the morale of the project team and too late when the project is out of control.

What are the options when a project isn't working?

1 **Go back a stage:** This is a major benefit of the work breakdown structure method of managing projects. If stakeholders are not fully satisfied at a milestone they can withhold funding for the next stage and insist that the previous stage is completed before moving on.

2 **Start again from scratch:** Clearly this is a drastic step. You also have to be confident that second time around there is a definite prospect of success.

3 **Kill it off:** Two of the skills a project leader needs are the objectivity and courage to kill a project off before it has become so expensive that no one dare stop it.

What causes a project to fail?

It seems that rarely a month goes by when we don't hear about a major IT project that has gone wrong, running over time and massively over budget. Of course there are many projects which succeed, coming in under time and under budget but these are few and far between. Research conducted among chief executives found that twice as many IT projects are considered to be unsuccessful than are considered successful. That's a fairly stunning proportion. Although no doubt there are degrees of failure within these that is still a shockingly poor record. It is also estimated that 15 per cent of all software development never delivers any benefit. But why? It appears that many projects have sown the seeds of their failure before they start. And a key word emerges here: communication.

The following extract from a case study sums up the problem rather well:

> '*A survey of more than 300 NHS staff in London showed that most workers are angry their views were not taken into account before the introduction of a system, which is aimed at improving information passed between hospitals and GPs. Trade union Amicus said its study showed lack of staff involvement was symptomatic of how the NHS is run. National officer Kevin Coyne said: "It's appalling that so many NHS staff lack confidence in the implementation of the world's largest*

civil IT project." Without consulting the people who will use these IT systems, the NHS management and IT providers will leave patients and NHS staff floundering in the dark.'

That final sentence should be a warning to all contemplating projects!

The most common causes of failure are:

- Poorly defined objectives
- Lack of end-user involvement
- Poor communication during the life of the project
- Unclear management structure
- Lack of leadership
- Poor planning.

Project planning tools: work breakdown structure

Work breakdown structure is the way in which projects are broken down into more easily managed phases. Each phase must achieve success criteria agreed at the outset by those involved in the project. If all criteria are fulfilled, funding for the next phase of the project is signed off and the next stage can begin. If there are problems these need to be fixed and seen to work before the next phase is given a green light. This way of working has the following benefits:

- It provides tight control over the project
- It makes the project team more focused
- It makes applying for approval of future projects easier.

Software for project planning

Microsoft Project helps project managers and business managers to manage schedules and resources. It provides timelines in graphic format so that the progress of a project is apparent at a glance. It does however require training to get the most out of it.

Attention checker quiz!

1 Who should decide which projects to tackle?

A Departmental managers ☐
B The IT Department ☐
C The Information Group ☐

2 Which of the following is not recommended as acategory for deciding on projects?

A Gaining industry leadership ☐
B Staying in the same place ☐
C Keeping the show on the road ☐

3 Project team members need to have two of these attributes – which two?

A Desire to see the project done the way they want ☐
B Able to anticipate problems ☐
C Politically astute ☐

4 Delegated project tasks can be allotted by:

A Giving them to someone who is already very busy ☐
B Giving them to someone who has nothing to do ☐
C Discussing the reasons for delegating responsibilities with the person who is to receive them and involving the project team in the discussion ☐

5 The best way for the project team to communicate is by:

A Face-to-face meetings ☐
B Email ☐
C Phone ☐
D All of the above – especially face-to-face meetings ☐

6 Which of the following is essential for a successful project?

A Lack of end user involvement ☐
B Make the objectives crystal clear in advance ☐
C Management should stand back from any involvement ☐

Appendices

In this section you will find:

- **a: sample information strategy**
- **b: best practice**
- **c: glossary of terms**

A: Sample information strategy

This appendix presents a sample information strategy for an advertising agency.

1.0 Executive summary

Conclusions

- Agency X's campaign processes lend themselves to automated workflow.
- Agency X would achieve significant savings by implementing a workflow system and an information centre to service clients more efficiently and cost effectively.
- The culture of the company lends itself to the effective use of information.
- Information must be managed effectively, kept fresh, accurate and it must be clear whose responsibility this is.
- An Information Group will be formed to instigate, manage and measure information development.
- Hardware, software and network design will be upgraded in line with the business plan and budgets.
- Supplier agreements will be renegotiated to drive down costs.
- Four complementary major developments over the next 24 months will give Agency X competitive advantage. These will be:
  - Knowledge management tools
  - Automated campaign workflow and online approval of work
  - An online library of the agency's creative work
  - An information centre for clients, partners and suppliers to collaborate with the agency.

Business benefits

- Better client service
- Reduction in administration element of campaigns
- Higher profile of the agency with existing and potential clients
- Increased profit margins
- Tighter control of costs.

Implications

- The agency's present work processes will be radically changed by use of a central information resource.
- Relationships with clients and suppliers will become closer as organizational boundaries become blurred.
- The organization will move from a knowledge hoarding to a knowledge sharing culture.

2.0 Aims and objectives

The aim of this report is to provide a roadmap for technological innovation within Agency X and between Agency X, clients, partners and suppliers. Any innovation must be sympathetic to the culture of the agency and bring demonstrable business benefits to the organization.

Things should only be done that:

- Make a significant contribution to the achievement of the business plan.
- Will pay for themselves in a reasonable and predetermined time.
- Can be explained in simple language to those who will need to make them work.

Business objectives 2001

1 To achieve incremental income growth of £2.5m over budget.
2 To improve client retention by more closely auditing the health

and effectiveness of relationships ensuring that smaller clients feel they are getting the same quality of service as larger ones.

3 To maintain the emphasis on our creative standards, prioritizing investment in creative disciplines.
4 To become the lead European player in Agency Z Worldwide, securing three international clients.
5 To implement a comprehensive upgrade of IT and knowledge management systems.

3.0 Introduction and background

Agency X is the 15th largest advertising agency by billings in the UK, a position it has achieved through organic growth in the last few years. Part of a worldwide agency network, it is a wholly owned subsidiary of Agency Y, a global media group and has a blue-chip client roster. In addition to these few highly profitable accounts, the agency also services a large number of small to medium-sized clients. These are less profitable as the agency strives to provide a similar degree of quality and commitment to their brand management thus incurring high costs on lower billing figures.

4.0 Present situation

4.1 Information technology infrastructure

- The IT function needs strengthening to support staff in an effective manner. Procurement procedures are inefficient and unable to deliver hardware and software on time. Historically this has created frustration among staff in the agency.
- IT provision and support is outsourced and although the outsourcing company has created a temporarily stable network environment it is not within the scope of their contract nor do they have the skills to contribute to strategic vision. This leaves a planning vacuum with the following outcomes:
  - There is no clear step-by-step approach to IT development and little prospect of gaining competitive advantage.

- Each department orders its own software through the outsourcing company resulting in no economy of scale (for example a Microsoft agreement could bring a 25 per cent discount).

Due to this haphazard approach departments and staff within departments are on different versions of software, leading to instability of systems and making upgrades more costly and difficult to manage. There is also a likelihood that these systems will not work with future developments.

Likewise on the hardware front there is no incentive for the supplier to pursue best deals. Yet with recession affecting many major technology providers, now is the perfect time to strike hard bargains and invest cost-effectively for the agency's future.

- There are fundamental problems with the way in which the network is wired. These it must be stressed are not of the outsourcing company's making but rather as a result of misdirected cost-cutting when the present building was occupied.
- Desktop computers are of widely varying age and quality and the company is paying too much for its hardware.
- Software versions are many and varied.
- The main network computers are getting old and are running an old version of a network operating system resulting in regular loss of network services to staff.
- There is little in the way of security and areas of especial concern are Internet email which arrives untouched by virus checking and the lack of a reliable backup system. These are time bombs which could have serious consequences for the agency if not tackled immediately.
- There is no disaster recovery plan in place.

4.2 Client service

A problem with client retention has been identified. As one director put it, '*We're great at courtship and foreplay but when it comes to marriage we get bored and lose interest.*' This is reflected in the roller coaster nature of billings year on year. The company will benefit from involving the client more actively in campaigns, identifying how the admin element of client service can be drastically cut and the whole thing made more rewarding for agency staff and client.

4.3 Internal effectiveness

Throughout the agency procedures have become cumbersome with much duplication of work. An example of this is management information. To discover the performance of the top five clients takes three days and involves a long chain of people. This hampers high level decision making in the agency. The structure of the company, with departments operating primarily in an autonomous fashion, hinders communication and the spread of best practice. Useful information is often stranded in 'knowledge cul-de-sacs' or in inaccessible formats.

4.4 Business innovation

Business innovation means the use of technology to develop new working practices and competencies to create competitive advantage. Within the agency there is a willingness to innovate but no framework within which to do so. The following headings help focus on where business innovation can have most influence.

Technology clients

We work with several clients whose core activity is development and provision of technology products and services. An understanding of innovation is essential so that account teams feel comfortable with the background technology, understand the products thoroughly and can plan and produce work backed by a sound understanding of the markets in which these clients operate.

Clients' own use of technology

To compete in a market where clients are more aware of technology and its advantages, Agency X needs to use innovation to attract new clients, improve service to existing ones and be seen as a leading edge agency. Where a client has limited technology capability of its own, Agency X may be able, for a fee, to host systems of benefit to the client or offer advice and demonstrate the effectiveness of solutions through our own experience.

Suppliers

Business innovation is also a way of establishing direct links with trading partners. Through online procurement we can significantly reduce costs and gain more control over purchasing. For example the policy of buying online with Dell has significantly reduced hardware costs.*

5.0 Information vision and architecture

5.1 Information mission statement

The mission of Information Services and the Information Group is to meet the objectives in the business plan to support the strategic values and objectives of the company and to provide reliable information services to all clients, both within and where appropriate, outside the company.

To achieve this it will be necessary to identify new tools that enable management to increase their effectiveness in operating and managing the business.

5.2 Information vision

- Existing campaign processes will be automated where possible to reduce admin and free time of account handlers.
- Management will have instant access to information required to operate and manage the business effectively.
- All staff will have high-speed access to the Internet for research and communication.
- The corporate network will be extended via the Internet to encompass clients, suppliers and partner agencies in providing a high quality service to clients.
- The corporate network will be able to support a large number of remote staff allowing creative teams to work more flexibly with access to the company's online digital library and workflow system.
- To become the lead European player in Agency Z Worldwide, securing three international clients. Development of a secure

global electronic network will give access to valuable resources across and between group companies.

- Staff will have software tools to make all information easily accessible.
- The corporate network will be able to send and receive large files from clients at high speed.
- Clients will be able to access the agency information library through mobile devices.

5.3 Information architecture

Technology component

- The entire information creation process must be supported by an excellent technical infrastructure.
- Critical data will always be stored in a secure place and backed up daily.
- All company staff will be attached to a high-speed electronic network that provides easy access to a variety of information and computing resources both within and outside the company.
- All information systems that contain or use critical information will be available on the electronic network.
- All hardware and software will be selected from a list of approved systems maintained by the Information Group.
- The Information Group will maintain a list of supported email, word processing, spreadsheet and analytical software.
- The Information Group will maintain a list of supported hardware and operating systems.
- The Information Group will define and publish information collection and maintenance standards.

Human component

- The Information Group will be chaired by the MD and will consist of Department Heads and the IT Manager.
- The Information Group will have overall responsibility for

quality of information in the company.

- The Information Group will be responsible for ensuring that IT purchases comply with the IT architecture.
- The Information Group will be responsible for approving departmental IT budgets.
- Each manager in the company will be responsible for outlining a departmental information systems plan and budget with assistance form the Information Group.
- Every member of staff will have at least 24 hours of IT training per year.
- Clients may access the information stored in a secure area of our system.

6.0 Strategic information systems plan

6.1 Strategy agenda

- Manage development of network architecture and security in accordance with business and staff requirements.
- Help departments build individual information plans using the Information Services Department's expertise and knowledge and in accordance with the Information Group's guidelines.
- Create and maintain a shortlist of approved hardware and software that can be efficiently used within the network design to meet staff requirements.
- Coordinate with other departments through the Information Group in the evaluation and design of information and communication systems to meet the company's strategic and business needs.
- Provide and annually update a prioritized list of sources for external data and information that will strategically help the company.
- Encourage active staff and client participation in information use through training programmes and help sessions.

6.2 Strategy objectives

- Use IT to reduce our clients' cost of doing business with us.
- Provide unique information and knowledge to clients that will increase loyalty to our service.
- Use IT to increase our clients' costs of switching to a new agency.
- Use internal and external information sources to learn more about our clients and possible market niches.
- Use IT to help our clients increase their revenues.

7.0 Long-term operational information systems plan

7.1 Knowledge management product: *Alchemist* (powered by Autonomy)

What does it do?

Alchemist searches, retrieves, centralizes and catalogues all relevant information from internal and external sources.

Example: Provides instant retrieval of a PowerPoint presentation on the UK car market by a staff member who left three years ago and links it with marketing figures found on a car company's corporate website.

Business benefits:

- Transforms low value raw data into valuable information.
- Reduces the incidence of reinventing the wheel.
- Captures intellectual property value (stops the '90 per cent of company's value walks out the door every evening' syndrome).
- Improves the training capability of the company.
- Improves client service.

Alchemist Bronze: Collects data

Alchemist Silver: Interprets and contextualizes data to create information

Alchemist Gold: Reframes information into knowledge. After this point it is made available for general consumption internally, repackaged and sold to clients.

Timescale: Twelve months.

7.2 Workflow management product: *Magnifi*

What does it do?

Magnifi is an electronic job-bag reducing waste, time and cost associated with running a campaign. When linked to the client their campaign becomes to an extent self-servicing with, for example, viewing and discussion of creative briefs and minor artwork amendments, all conducted online. For clients and account handlers, the part of the campaign they really dislike is the mind numbing bureaucracy of form filling, exchanging (and losing) faxes etc. With online servicing and tracking of work this element is removed and it avoids minor problems becoming major issues. Although the dry admin side is greatly lessened, the face-to-face aspect of client service should not be forgotten. There is an argument that says if paperwork and office work is reduced then account handlers will have more time for face-to-face contact with the client.

Better management

Account Directors and clients can see exactly how a campaign is progressing with overdue work highlighted in red. They can then identify whether the delay is within the agency or elsewhere. Coupled with artwork online they are able to view work for approval and approve it electronically if they so wish. The campaign cannot be closed until client and agency have made their comments on where it could be improved.

Business benefits:

- More efficient control of campaigns.
- Reduced errors and improved client service.
- Increased teamwork with clients.
- Reduced cost of campaigns (couriers/phone/fax).
- Increased barriers to exit for client.

- Valuable information and knowledge captured from campaigns and fed into Alchemist system.

Timescale: Eighteen months.

7.3 Digital asset library: *AdLib*

What does it do?

Catalogues all the company's TV, Press, Outdoor, Cinema and Interactive commercials attaching information such as director, creative team, music and end line to the work which can be played or viewed online and saved into a showreel. All these items are searchable; for instance if you are looking for a car ad directed by Tony Kaye you type the relevant details into a search box and the system will retrieve the work. A preview of the ad then lets you confirm if this is the work you want after which it can be downloaded or copied into a presentation.

Business benefits:

- A shop window for the agency.
- Reduces time wasted searching for archived advertisements.
- Ads can be found and copied and pasted into presentations with little effort.
- Lets creatives analyse previous campaigns and choose directors etc.
- Allows rapid creation of show reels for existing and prospective clients.
- Great for training. New staff can rapidly become familiar with the agency house style.
- Good for morale. Breaking work will be shown here – with an email alerting all staff to this.

Timescale: Eight months.

7.4 Information centre product: *Clinet*

What does it do?

Clinet is an Internet based information centre supplying information about the advertising industry to clients, partners, suppliers and the public. It will become a de facto standard source of knowledge and wisdom about the industry. There will be forums for people to comment – the aim is for it to become rather like *Campaign* but with a secure area for client discussion groups, share information and generally feel part of the Agency X community. This will tie them in more tightly to the agency and provide valuable feedback and insight into what they do and don't like about the agency.

Blue Velvet

This will be a 'light' version for mobile devices allowing clients to pick up information wherever they are. The appropriate contact(s) at every new client will be given a mobile handheld device as part of their induction pack when they join Agency X.

Business benefits:

- Higher profile with the general public and within the advertising industry.
- Attract more clients.
- Greatly improved client service.
- Additional revenue through general business consultancy service to clients.
- Increased fees from clients.

Timescale: Twenty-four months.

8.0 Short-term operational information systems plan

8.1 Information technology infrastructure

Information Group

An Information Group will be formed to drive and measure information development. The main task of the group will be to establish and communicate standards for hardware and software, identify IT developments that will bring competitive advantage, monitor current projects and set appropriate budgets based on department requirements. This group will have as its members the IT Director and Department Heads. It will be chaired by the Managing Director.

IT support team

Agency X has to regain control of IT provision and costs. This can only be done by bringing IT in-house, creating a client-service focused, well trained and highly motivated IT team.

Recommendation: Terminate ABC's contract and recruit a new team consisting of an IT Manager and three support staff with strong communications and people skills.

Internet email

The company is very exposed to destructive viruses from the Web and immediate implementation of Internet email virus checking is essential.

Recommendation: Subscribe to MessageLabs service which scans incoming and outgoing emails for potential viruses and quarantines them if found.

Network servers

The present servers are outdated and will not support the ambitions of the business for successful use of information. Storage is a constant problem with the servers running out of space on an almost daily basis.

Recommendation: Lease a new central server from Dell and implement modules of storage that can be attached without disrupting the network.

Desktop computers

If we are to gain competitive advantage through use of innovation, staff in the agency need the appropriate level of good quality computer that will help and not hinder them in their work.

Recommendation: Once the hardware audit is complete, identify staff who have not yet been provided with adequate hardware, assess their job function and install the appropriate computer for their needs.

Network cabling

The cabling in the building is badly designed and will not be able to support future developments.

Recommendation: Network performance would be greatly enhanced by installation of well planned and implemented cabling.

Hardware maintenance

The company is spending £14,000 per annum on a maintenance contract for desktop computers. Desktops are commodity items that rarely go wrong and usually only require cheap parts that can be kept on site.

Recommendation: Stop the maintenance contract for desktops. Investment saved can be spent on improving mission critical elements of the IT infrastructure such as servers or network cabling.

Operating systems

There has to be standardization of the operating system across the company to:

- Eliminate incompatibility between and within departments.
- Achieve economy of scale through buying in volume at one time.
- Make planning easier as upgrades will happen every three or four years.
- Reduce support and maintenance costs.

Disaster recovery

There is no disaster recovery plan in place and the agency is exposed to total data loss if the main fileserver were to fail as this is not adequately backed up. The priorities are:

- Identify, buy and install solid backup software and test regularly by restoring data onto a server.
- Develop a disaster recovery plan which will scale from minor incidents, such as loss of one server for a short period to complete loss of access to the building. Identify a disaster

recovery service that will allow the company to move key staff to another site where work can continue.

- Provide remote access to the network so that in the event of a major incident key staff can work from home.

Training

There is little point investing large sums of money in software and hardware if people are not trained to use it to its full potential.

Recommendation: Create a dedicated training area with six PCs and start weekly training sessions on the main software products. This will also be valuable for training staff as the new developments are implemented.

Noto

*The new Dell agreement removed two levels of price mark up firstly from the reseller and secondly from the outsourcing company cutting hardware costs in one instance by 70% but on average by around 30%.

B: Best practice

How to reduce your IT costs

1 Turn off non-essential computers at the end of the work day.

2 Turn off all monitors at night or activate the power saving function.

3 Plan your software and hardware purchasing for the year ahead.

4 If your company is part of a larger group negotiate group discounts with software providers.

5 Standardize hardware to reduce support costs.

6 Keep a small number of spares for standardized hardware.

7 Identify where maintenance agreements are required and terminate the ones that aren't.

8 Create software standards and buying policies. This also helps with budget planning.

9 If you have one or more remote offices use Voice over the Internet to reduce phone call charges.

10 Offer a 'finder's fee' for staff who introduce new recruits thereby reducing the high fees paid to a recruitment agency.

11 Create low cost extranets (secure sites with authorized access) for clients to view work in progress, cutting courier and fax costs.

12 Invoice via email.

How to add value through IT

Staff

1 Train staff in software to improve productivity.

2 Create an internal intranet for staff to exchange knowledge and ideas.

3 On the same intranet have discussion groups about the company – at times this may not be comfortable but you will learn a lot and you'll get some great ideas from the people who know the company best.

4 Create a technology showcase to try out and demonstrate new ideas.

Management

1 Give management access to information on your industry.

2 Provide information on competitors.

3 Make available information on potential clients.

4 General business information (a subscription to the *Economist* is a good starting point).

5 Supply management with frequent timely and accurate executive summaries of internal business information such as monthly sales figures or year-on-year revenue trends.

Clients

1 Find out what your clients are interested in and provide information.

2 Create an extranet for clients to access information on the projects you are doing for them.

3 Create a forum for clients to discuss your service or product (again you may get a few nasty surprises but wouldn't you rather they told you about problems with your product or service than potential clients?).

Suppliers

1 Involve your suppliers as you would any part of your company – it's quite likely they will be the people to get you out of a hole.

2 Find best prices via search functions on the Web.

3 Find alternative or substitute products on the Web.

4 Research the latest technology and its possible effects on your business or industry.

Others

1 Make your website *the* place to visit for information on your industry, offering helpful tips for finding the solutions your potential clients want – even if these are from competitors...

2 Create a site that is fun – provide competitions, pack the site with information and make it something people will return to again and again.

3 Identify where your business can benefit from using IT – are there new services or streams of revenue that you can generate?

4 Are there parts of your service that can be delivered over the Internet?

C: Glossary of terms

ADSL (Asymmetric Digital Subscriber Line) When we talk about consumer broadband, usually ADSL is what we mean. It is a way of connecting to the Internet over regular phone lines. The wires coming into your home or business are the same copper wires used for the regular phone service but they can support very fast transmission speeds. ADSL is the most common flavour but SDSL, which is faster, exists as well. DSL is now a popular alternative to *Leased Lines* and *ISDN*, being faster than ISDN and less costly than Leased Lines.

ARPANet (Advanced Research Projects Agency Network) The precursor to the *Internet*. Developed in the late 1960s and early 1970s by the US Department of Defence as an experiment in wide-area-networking that would survive a nuclear war.

See also: *Internet*

Backbone A high-speed line or series of connections that forms a major pathway within a network. The term is relative as a backbone in a small *network* will likely be much smaller than many non-backbone lines in a large network.

See also: *Network*

Bandwidth How much stuff you can send through a connection. Usually measured in bits-per-second. A full page of English text is about 16,000 bits. A fast modem can move about 15,000 bits in one second. Full-motion full-screen video would require roughly 10,000,000 bits-per-second, depending on compression.

See also: *Bit*

Bit (Binary DigIT) A single digit number in base-2, in other words, either a 1 or a zero. The smallest unit of computerized data. *Bandwidth* is usually measured in bits-per-second.

See also: *Bandwidth*, *Byte*, *Kilobyte*, *Megabyte*

Blog (web log) A blog can be in the form of a diary but often they are less structured comments and personal experiences that people write online.

Browser A program (software) that is used to look at various kinds of Internet resources.

Byte A set of *Bits* that represent a single character. Usually there are 8 Bits in a Byte, sometimes more, depending on how the measurement is being made.

See also: *Bit*

Client A software program that is used to contact and obtain data from a *Server* software program on another computer, often across a great distance. Each *Client* program is designed to work with one or more specific kinds of *Server* programs, and each *Server* requires a specific kind of *Client*. A Web *Browser* is a specific kind of *Client*.

Cookie The most common meaning of 'cookie' refers to a piece of information sent by a Web *Server* to a Web *Browser* that the *Browser* software is expected to save and to send back to the *Server* whenever the *Browser* makes additional requests from the *Server*. Cookies might contain information such as login or registration information, online 'shopping cart' information, user preferences, etc.

Cyberspace Term originated by author William Gibson in his novel *Neuromancer*, the word 'cyberspace' is currently used to describe the whole range of information resources available through computer networks.

Domain name The unique name that identifies an *Internet* site. For example www.ibm.com

Email (electronic mail) Messages, usually text, sent from one person to another via computer. Files of any sort, whether video, audio or text can also be attached to it. Email can also be sent automatically to a large number of addresses.

Ethernet A common method of connecting computers in a network. Ethernet will handle about 10,000,000 bits-per-second and can be used with almost any kind of computer.

Extranet A private network that a company or organization uses to share information with trusted clients and partners. Similar to an *Intranet*.

FAQ (Frequently Asked Questions) FAQs are documents that list and answer the most common questions on a particular subject.

Firewall A combination of hardware and software that separates a network into two or more parts for security purposes. Firewalls also protect company networks from unauthorized access via the *Internet* .

FTP (File Transfer Protocol) A very common method of moving files between two *Internet* sites.

Gateway The technical meaning is a hardware or software set-up that translates between two dissimilar protocols, for example Prodigy has a gateway that translates between its internal, proprietary email format and *Internet* email format. Another, sloppier meaning of gateway is to describe any mechanism for providing access to another system.

Gigabyte 1000 or 1024 *Megabytes*, depending on who is measuring.

See also: *Byte*, *Megabyte*

Hit Used in reference to the World Wide Web, 'hit' means a single viewing by someone browsing.

Home page (or **Homepage**) The main web page for a business, organization.

Host Any computer on a *network* that is a repository for services available to other computers on the *network*. It is quite common to have one host machine provide several services, such as *WWW* and *USENET*.

HTML (HyperText Markup Language) The coding system used to create *Hypertext* documents for use on the *World Wide Web*.

HTTP (HyperText Transfer Protocol) The protocol for moving *hypertext* files across the *Internet*. HTTP is the most important protocol used in the *World Wide Web*.

Internet The vast collection of inter-connected networks that all use the *TCP/IP* protocols and that evolved from the *ARPANET* of the late 1960s and early 1970s.

Intranet A private network inside a company or organization that uses the same kinds of software that you would find on the public *Internet* to publish information for internal use only.

IP Address A unique number consisting of 4 parts separated by dots, e.g. 165.113.245.2. Rather like a postcode every machine that is on the *Internet* has a unique IP address.

ISDN (Integrated Services Digital Network) Basically a way to move more data over existing regular phone lines. ISDN is rapidly becoming available to much of the USA and in most markets it is priced very comparably to standard analog phone circuits. It can provide speeds of roughly 128,000 bits-per-second over regular phone lines. In practice, most people will be limited to 56,000 or 64,000 bits-per-second.

ISP (Internet Service Provider) A company that provides access to the *Internet* . For example BT or AOL.

Java A programming language invented by Sun Microsystems that is specifically designed for writing programs that can be safely downloaded to your computer through the *Internet* and immediately run without fear of viruses or other harm to your computer or files. Using small Java programs (called 'Applets'), web pages can include functions such as animations, calculators, and other clever tricks.

JPEG (Joint Photographic Experts Group) Most commonly mentioned as a format for image files. JPEG format is preferred to the GIF format for photographic images as opposed to line art or simple logo art.

Kilobyte A thousand bytes. Actually, usually 1024 (2^10) bytes.

LAN (Local Area Network) A computer network limited to the immediate area, usually the same building or floor of a building.

Leased line Refers to a phone line that is rented for exclusive 24-hour, 7-days-a-week use from your location to another location. The highest speed data connections require a leased line.

Login Noun or a verb. Noun: The account name used to gain access to a computer system. Not a secret (contrast with *Password*). Verb: The act of entering into a computer system.

Megabyte A million *bytes*. Technically, 1024 *kilobytes*.

Modem (MOdulator, DEModulator) A device that connects your computer through a phone line, allowing it to communicate with other computers through the phone system. The computer has to dial up to start a session, unlike with ADSL where the connection is always on. In effect modems do for computers what a telephone does for humans.

Network Any time you connect two or more computers together so that they can share resources, you have a computer network. Connect two or more networks together and you have an *Internet* .

Password A code used to gain access to a locked system. Good passwords contain letters and non-letters and are not simple combinations such as *virtue7*. A good one might be: Hot$1-6

Portal A website that is or is intended to be the first place people see when using the Web. Typically a portal site has a catalog of websites, a search engine, or both. A portal site may also offer *email* and other services to entice people to use that site as their main 'point of entry' (hence 'portal') to the Web. Examples are Yahoo! or AOL.

Router A special-purpose computer (or software package) that connects two or more networks. Routers spend all their time looking at the destination addresses of the information passing through them and deciding which route to send them on.

Security certificate A chunk of information (often stored as a text file) that is used by the *SSL* protocol to establish a secure connection.

Server A computer that provides a specific kind of service to other computers, e.g. email server, print server, file server. A single server machine usually provides a number of services to *clients* on the *network*.

Spam (or **Spamming**) An inappropriate use of email to send the same message to a large number of people who didn't ask for it.

SQL (Structured Query Language) A specialized programming language for sending queries to databases. Most industrial-strength and many smaller database applications can be addressed using SQL. Each specific application will have its own version of SQL implementing features unique to that application, but all SQL-capable databases support a common subset of SQL.

SSL (Secure Sockets Layer) A security standard designed to enable safe communications across the Internet. SSL is used mostly (but not exclusively) in communications between web *Browsers* and Web *Servers*. It is essential for financial transaction on the *Internet* .

TCP/IP (Transmission Control Protocol/Internet Protocol) This is the suite of protocols that defines the *Internet*.

Terabyte 1000 *gigabytes*.

UNIX A computer operating system (the basic software running on a computer, underneath things like word processors and spreadsheets). UNIX is designed to be used by many people at the same time (it is multi-user) and has *TCP/IP* built-in. It is the most common operating system for *servers* on the *Internet*.

URL (Uniform Resource Locator) The standard way to give the address of any resource on the *Internet*. A URL for a website looks like this: www.hoddereducation.co.uk

VPN (Virtual Private Network) Usually refers to a *network* in which some of the parts are connected using the public *Internet*, but the data sent across the *Internet* is encrypted, so the entire network is 'virtually' private. A typical example would be a company *Network* where there are two offices in different cities. Using the *Internet* the two offices merge their *Networks* into one network, but encrypt traffic that uses the *Internet* link.

WAN (Wide Area Network) Any *Internet* or *network* that covers an area larger than a single building or campus.

WWW (World Wide Web) Frequently used (incorrectly) when referring to 'The Internet', WWW has two major meanings. First, loosely used: the whole constellation of resources that can be accessed using *Gopher*, *FTP*, *HTTP*, *telnet*, *USENET*, *WAIS* and some other tools. Second, the universe of hypertext servers (*HTTP servers*) which are the servers that allow text, graphics, sound files, etc. to be mixed together.

ZIP Drive Versatile, portable, compatible, cost-effective magnetic storage for all your critical files.

Further reading

Background to e-commerce and extranets

Hagel, J. and Armstrong, A. (1997) *Net Gain. Expanding markets through virtual communities*. Harvard Business School Press.

Inmon, W.H., Imhoff, C. and Sousa, R. (1998) *Corporate Information Factory*. Wiley Computer Publishing.

Kosiur, D. (1997) *Understanding Electronic Commerce*. Microsoft Press.

Papows, J. (1999) *Enterprise.com. Market leadership in the information age*. Nicholas Brealey Publishing.

Timmers, P. (1999) *Electronic Commerce. Strategies and models for Business-to-Business Trading*. Wiley.

Technology management

Earl, M.J. (1989) *Management Strategies for Information Technology*. Prentice Hall International.

Mabey, C. and Mayon-White, B. (1993) *Managing Change*. Paul Chapman Publishing.

Mankin, D., Cohen, S.G. and Bikson, T.K. (1996) *Teams and Technology*. Harvard Business School Press.

Marchand, D., Kettinger, W. and Rollins, J. (2001) *Making the Invisible Visible*. John Wiley and Sons Ltd.

Moore, G. (1991) *Crossing the Chasm*. Harper Business.

Moore, G. (1995) *Inside the Tornado*. Harper Business.

Rhodes, E. and Wield, D. (1994) *Implementing New Technologies*. NCC Blackwell.

Wainwright, Martin E., DeHayes, D.W., Hoffer, J.A. and Perkins, W.C. (2001) *Managing Information Technology. What Managers Need to Know*. Prentice Hall.

General reading

Drucker, P. (1999) *Management Challenges for the 21st Century*. Butterworth Heinemann.

Gates, B. (1995) *The Road Ahead*. Penguin.

Negroponte, N. (1995) *Being Digital*. Coronet Books

Peters, T. (1994) *The Pursuit of WOW!* Macmillan.

Peters, T. (1999) *Professional Service Firm 50*. Knopf

Journals

Peet, J. 'Define and sell, E-commerce survey', *The Economist*, 26 February–3 March 2000, pp 6–9.

Reports

Guptill, B. and Terhune, A., *Managing ROI for Extranet Projects*, Gartner Group

Releasing the value of knowledge (2000), A Cranfield School of Management and Microsoft survey of UK industry.

Other helpful sources of information

Hardware

Dell Outlet Store: www.dell.co.uk

Software

Sophos (anti-virus software): http://www.sophos.com

Microsoft Licensing: www.microsoft.com/uk/licensing/

Services

Insight (hardware and software): http://uk.insight.com

Capital Continuity (real time server protection): http://www.capitalcontinuity.co.uk/index.asp

Skype (free and low cost Internet phone calls): www.skype.com

The Pagan Consultancy (information security and ISO27001 auditing): www.thepaganconsultancy.com

Technical

TechRepublic (the latest on information technology and informative papers): http://techrepublic.com.com/

ZDNet (reviews of products plus business and IT advice): http://www.zdnet.com/

index